The Flemish Parliament

THE FLEMISH PARLIAMENT

TEXT **MARTINE GOOSSENS**
PHOTOGRAPHY **MARNIX VAN ESBROECK**

lannoo

FLEMISH PARLIAMENT

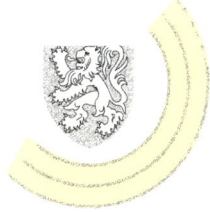

THIS BOOK IS PUBLISHED BY LANNOO
UNDER THE AUSPICES OF THE FLEMISH PARLIAMENT
ON THE OCCASION OF
ITS TWENTY-FIFTH ANNIVERSARY

Contents

A glass house
in the heart of Brussels

The weekend *of 16th and 17th March 1996 was an historical moment for Flanders: it was the occasion of the official opening ceremony of the Flemish Parliament building in the heart of Brussels. The Flemish Parliament, which had been directly elected for the first time on 21st May 1995, was now holding its first meeting in its own chamber. There were six thousand Flemings with ringside seats to assist in the opening of the building. Since then the Flemish Parliament building has received about two hundred visitors a day. This building is clearly a new attraction in Brussels.*

The Flemish Parliament building is interesting in many respects. It has a long historical background, going back to the end of the eighteenth century. It was then that the Warande district was developed round the Brussels Park. A prestigious concert hall and ballroom called the Edel-Concert rose on the corner of the Hertogstraat and the Leuvenseweg, and was a great credit to the sophisticated style of the district. After Belgian independence, the building was the temporary home to a Freemasons' lodge and several ministerial departments. In 1905, on the site of the former concert hall, the stately new Hôtel des Postes et de la Marine was erected, the headquarters of the Post Office's executive committee and the Office of Maritime Affairs. This building formed part of the 'ministry district' that developed round the Palace of the Nation in the second half of the nineteenth century. The 'Post Office building' retained this function until 1987, when it was bought by the Flemish Parliament, then called the Flemish Council, for conversion into a functional modern parliament building. The building still bears many traces of its past history and this is precisely one of its charms.

By contrast with the building, the Flemish Parliament itself is a recent institution. Its history only began in 1971. Between 1971

◄

The office of the Speaker of the Flemish Parliament, in the finely restored council chamber of the former 'Hôtel des Postes et de la Marine'.

and 1996 the Flemish parliamentary assembly expanded from a modest cultural parliament, with limited authority, into a fully-fledged parliament for the Flemish people. Thanks to the Flemish Parliament (this has been its official title since 13th June 1995), Flanders now possesses major advantages when it comes to taking control of its own future and building a democratic and socially just community. It is the responsibility of the 124 Flemish Members of Parliament to live up to this challenge and to provide a genuine solution for the many social problems facing Flanders on the eve of the twenty-first century.

I am convinced that in the years and decades to come, even more than over the last twenty-five years, the Flemish Parliament will set Flanders' social course. It will all happen in the Flemish Parliament building, a glass house in the heart of Brussels, where the Flemish Members of Parliament wish to practice politics in all openness.

The publishers Lannoo have taken the initiative of publishing an illustrated book on the occasion of the twenty-fifth anniversary of the Flemish Parliament. The Bureau considered this a good idea because it is an effective way of making the building and the institution better known both at home and abroad. I hope this book will prompt many Flemish people to visit their parliament. Just drop into the Flemish Parliament building and get to know the place where the Flemish Members of Parliament work, it will definitely be an instructive experience.

Play of light and shadow on and through the glass floor above The Shell.

▶

Norbert De Batselier,
Speaker of the Flemish Parliament.

1

Historical outline of the Flemish Parliament

The Flemish Parliament is a recent institution. Its history is inseparably linked to the transformation of the unitary Belgian state into a federal state, a process that was set in motion in 1970 and today is still not yet entirely complete. The authority as well as the political importance of the Flemish Parliament also increased in parallel with the development of the federal state. Today, the Flemish Parliament has become a fully-fledged parliament for the Flemish people.

The first parliament for the Flemings:
an institution with limited authority (1971-1980)

THE HISTORICAL BACKGROUND

The Belgian state, which was set up in 1830, was a *unitary state*: all the subjects of the new kingdom were governed by one central political authority, embodied in one national parliament and one national government. The laws made by the Belgian national parliament applied to all Belgians, and the ministers in the national government exercised their authority over the whole territory of Belgium. The founders of this unitary state simply assumed that all the inhabitants of the new state felt 'Belgian'. There was no mention of the notion 'Fleming' or 'Walloon' as such. French was, as if self-evidently, the only official language, and was to symbolize the unity of the new state.

And yet the character of the new Belgian state was essentially heterogeneous. The Flemish provinces lived principally from agriculture; Dutch dialects formed the language of the people there. The Walloon provinces were oriented more towards industry and mining; the dialects in their region leaned towards French. Historical and cultural reasons had also led to French becoming the cultured language of the 'upper' social classes in the Flemish provinces. Dutch, the language of the people in the Flemish provinces, was not considered a full and proper language in those circles, and so administration and the law had to a great extent been transferred into French.

This discrimination was to lead, very soon after independence, to the growth of the first great field of tension in the Belgian state: tension between the defenders of the homogeneous French-speaking Belgian state and the *Flemish Movement*, which was struggling for the acknowledgement of Dutch as a full and official language alongside French. The *language conflict* that arose out of this shed the first doubts on the ideal picture of the unitary Belgian state.

At twilight the reflection of daylight off the dome diminishes and the lights of the Domed Hall become visible...

By means of a series of *language laws*, The Belgian state succeeded in temporarily reconciling the two language groups. The first language law, in 1873, obliged the legal system in Flanders and Brussels to use Dutch in all cases where it had not been established that the defendant spoke French. When this law had finally been passed, after laborious debates, it opened the door to laws on the use of Dutch in public administration (1878) and in higher education (1888). In 1898 parliament passed the *Equality Act*, which put Dutch on the same official footing as French. However, compliance with the language laws was by no means universal, and the Flemish Movement unremittingly continued its struggle for the acknowledgement of Dutch.

The language conflict flared up again after the Second World War. It often led to incidents, particularly in Brussels. Brussels had originally been a Flemish city, but the Flemings had to look on in distress while the Belgian

For twenty-five years, from December 1971 to March 1996, the Flemish Parliament met in the rooms of the Lower House in the Palace of the Nation.

capital rapidly became French-speaking. The 1846 census showed that almost 67% of the inhabitants of Brussels were still Dutch-speaking, but by 1947 this had decreased to 24%. The insidious influence of French-speakers in the Flemish boroughs surrounding Brussels was also a thorn in the Flemish side. In the sixties and seventies in particular, Brussels was to expand into one of the greatest points of conflict between the Flemish and Walloon communities.

After the Second World War a series of new tensions grew up between the Flemish and the Walloons, in addition to the language conflict, ones that could no longer be solved by language laws alone.

The most significant source of new tension was the shift of the economic centre of gravity from Wallony to Flanders. Throughout the nineteenth century Flanders had been a predominantly rural area with a low standard of living. Now, thanks in part to the expansion laws passed in the sixties, it was undergoing remarkable economic growth. The port of Antwerp became a magnet for new industries, and new companies established themselves all over the Flemish provinces. This was in great contrast to the decline of the

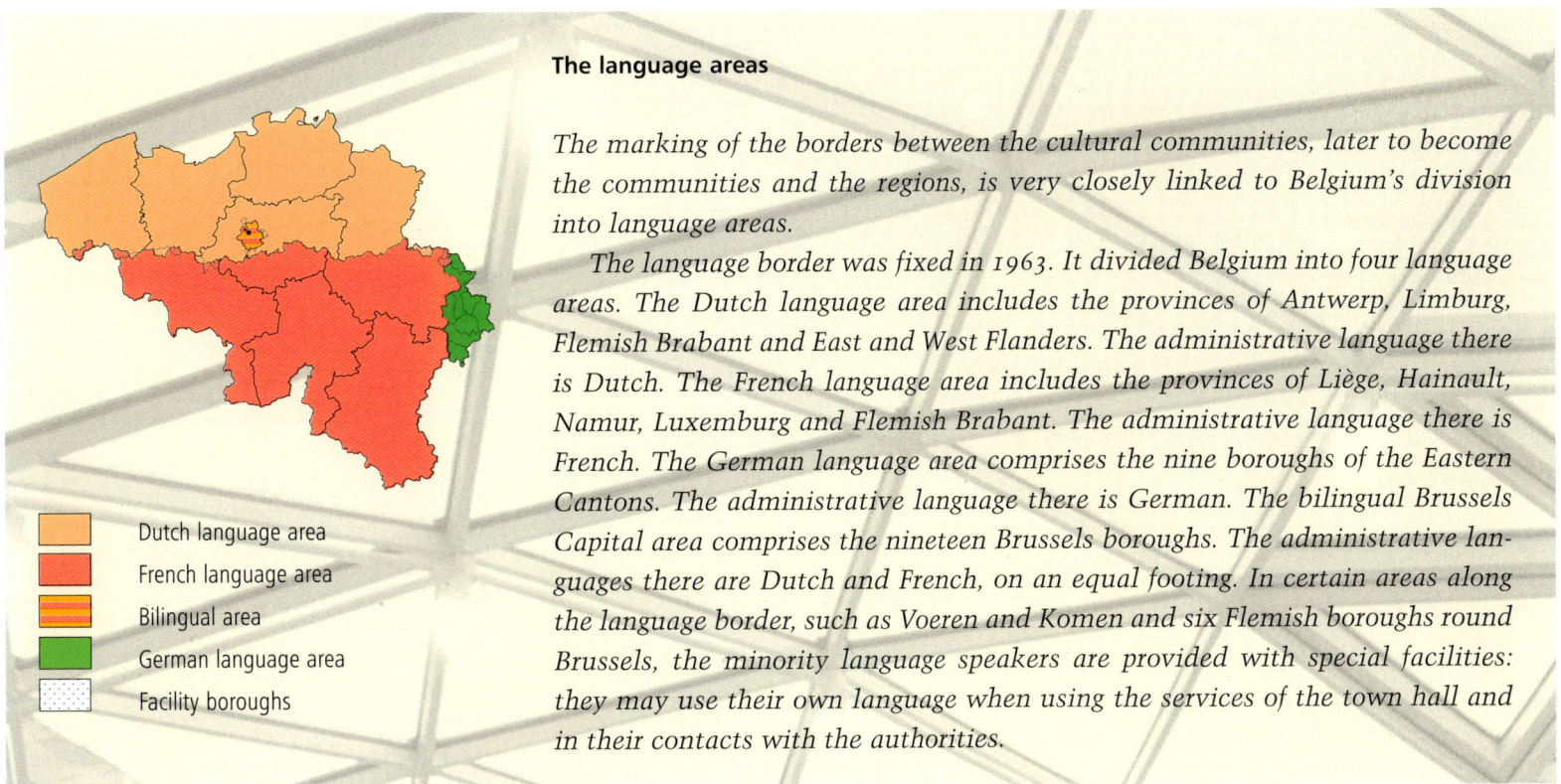

- Dutch language area
- French language area
- Bilingual area
- German language area
- Facility boroughs

The language areas

The marking of the borders between the cultural communities, later to become the communities and the regions, is very closely linked to Belgium's division into language areas.

The language border was fixed in 1963. It divided Belgium into four language areas. The Dutch language area includes the provinces of Antwerp, Limburg, Flemish Brabant and East and West Flanders. The administrative language there is Dutch. The French language area includes the provinces of Liège, Hainault, Namur, Luxemburg and Flemish Brabant. The administrative language there is French. The German language area comprises the nine boroughs of the Eastern Cantons. The administrative language there is German. The bilingual Brussels Capital area comprises the nineteen Brussels boroughs. The administrative languages there are Dutch and French, on an equal footing. In certain areas along the language border, such as Voeren and Komen and six Flemish boroughs round Brussels, the minority language speakers are provided with special facilities: they may use their own language when using the services of the town hall and in their contacts with the authorities.

Walloon industrial basin. At the end of the eighteenth century Wallony had been the birthplace of the Industrial Revolution on the European Continent. Now it was seeing the largest industries of yesteryear going under, and watched with sorrow as the previously poor Flanders expanded into Belgium's economic leader. The fear grew in Wallony that its chances of survival within the Belgian state were diminishing as a result of that state providing insufficient help for the flagging Walloon industry. Wallony pressed for *economic self-rule*: it wanted to keep the levers of economic policy in its own hands.

On the other side there was the increasing self-confidence of the leading industrial and political circles in Flanders. The conversion of the education system to the Dutch language began to bear fruit. A Flemish-minded elite gradually came into being, which not only worked for the application and expansion of the language laws, but which also stood up for Flanders' *cultural self-rule*, together with the Flemish Movement.

Lastly, there were the typical postwar issues that were judged differently in Flanders than in Wallony. The divergent reactions of Flanders and Wallony to sensitive political issues like the Repression (1945-1950), the Royal Question (1945-1950) and the Act of Unity (1961) indicated a deep political and mental rift between the north and south of the country. The language conflict between the Flemish and the Walloons had in other words escalated into a clash between two models of society, a full *community conflict*. The birth of 'community' parties such as the Volksunie (VU) in 1954, the Front des Francophones (FDF) in 1965, the Rassemblement Wallon (RW) in 1968, and the division of the traditional political parties into Flemish and Walloon wings – CVP/PSC in 1968, PVV/PRL in 1971 and the BSP/PSB in 1978 – were the most striking political manifestations of this.

THE 1970 CONSTITUTIONAL REVISION

There was a gradual but steady growth of the understanding that Belgium could only be saved by the *reorganization of Belgium into a federal state*, whereby the Flemish and the Walloons would each be given a certain form of political autonomy. In 1970 parliament took an initial modest step in this direction: Belgium was divided into three *cultural communities* corresponding to the three largest language areas in the country – the Dutch, French and German cultural communities – and three *regions* – Flanders, Wallony and Brussels – which were to assume a number of powers from the central Belgian level of administration, in the fields of culture and economy.

Roger Raveel was commissioned to design a work of art for the broad area in front of the Speaker's office. It is a monumental work entitled 'Reflection on the illusion of power', using oil paint on canvas, mirrors and mixed media. The photographer's viewpoint emphasizes the trompe l'oeil: while the right-hand door of the office is open at the top, the lower part appears to be closed. But the lower part reflects the closed left-hand door of the office.

▶

The formation of the regions was for the time being not actually carried out, however. This was because the Flemish and the Walloons did not agree on the boundaries of the Brussels region, which was dominated by the French language group. Flanders considered that Brussels should remain restricted to the nineteen boroughs of the Brussels district and could never become a full region alongside Flanders and Wallony. The Flemish were afraid that they would be forced into a minority position in any such threefold system. Conversely, the French-speakers *did* want Brussels to be a fully-fledged third region, and that the Brussels region would even be expanded by the inclusion of a number of peripheral Flemish boroughs. In the end it was 1988 before the Brussels region assumed its definitive form.

The division into cultural communities *did* take place in 1970. The two largest cultural communities in the country, the Dutch and the French, were both given a limited form of political self-rule. This assumed concrete form in the establishment of parliaments for these cultural communities. These parliaments took over the legislative powers of the national parliament in cultural and language affairs – areas in which the two communities had been clashing for decades. *This signified the break-up of the 'legislative monopoly' of the Belgian Parliament, and at the same time heralded the end of the unitary Belgian state.* The constitutional amendments of 1980, 1988 and 1993 were additional deliberate steps in the direction set in 1970.

We observe that no Brussels cultural community and therefore no Brussels cultural parliament were established in 1970: the Flemish and the Walloons agreed that no such Brussels cultural community existed, and that they would have to manage cultural affairs in Brussels between them. In concrete terms, this meant that the monolingual Dutch cultural institutions in Brussels would come under the authority of the Flemish cultural parliament, and the monolingual French under the authority of the French cultural parliament. The bilingual cultural institutions remained under the authority of the national parliament.

THE FLEMINGS' CULTURAL PARLIAMENT, 1971-1980

An incomplete parliament

The first Flemish parliament was officially entitled the *Cultural Council for the Dutch Cultural Community*. Since its powers were chiefly cultural, it was called a cultural parliament. It was in fact a parliamentary assembly, but by no means a fully-fledged parliament.

It was a parliament because it could pass decrees with the force of law. These *decrees* or Flemish laws applied only to members of the Dutch Cultural Community. The laws of the Belgian parliament could not change or abolish these decrees.

One of the first limitations of the real power of the Flemish cultural parliament was that it could only pass decrees in a limited number of areas of competence. These where chiefly cultural and language affairs. Compared to the total range of authority of the Belgian state, this was very modest: economy and employment, environmental planning, traffic and home affairs, to name but a few, all remained under the authority of the national parliament.

Furthermore, the Flemish cultural parliament did not have the power to appoint its own ministers to implement the decrees passed. Flanders did not get a government of its own. These were ministers from the national government charged with implementing the decrees of the Flemish cultural parliament. In concrete terms this meant that certain decrees passed by the cultural parliament were in fact never implemented.

And lastly it appeared from the composition of the cultural parliament that it was not a full parliament: it was not directly elected, but assembled from the Dutch-speaking members of the lower and upper houses of the Belgian state. This was the basis of the so-called *double mandate* which was to remain in existence until the first direct elections to the Flemish parliament in 1995, and which between 1971 and 1995 formed a genuine hindrance to its proper operation. The members had to divide their time between the national and the Flemish parliament, which often led to organizational problems including an overlapping of activities. The double mandate also had a significant psychological disadvantage: the members felt first and foremost members of the Belgian parliament, and only in the second, and often subordinate, place members of the Flemish parliament. After all, they were not directly elected to the latter institution. This feeling led to the interests of the Belgian state taking precedence over those of the Dutch Cultural Community in the minds of many of its members. Even more pernicious was the fact that membership of the Flemish parliament was imposed, and derived from the

The symbols of the Flemish Community

The Raskin decree issued on 6th July 1973 granted the Flemish Cultural Community its own symbols: as its flag 'A lion d'or, on sable, with claws and tongue of gules', as its anthem 'the first two verses of the Lion of Flanders, text by Hippoliet van Peene and music by Karel Miry', and an annual holiday on 11th July. A decree of 13th April 1988 abolished the Raskin decree and replaced it with the decree 'for the establishment of the coat of arms, flag, anthem and holiday of the Flemish Community'. In this decree the coat of arms of the Flemish Community, which was missing from the Raskin decree, was established as 'A crowned lion d'or, on sable, with claws and tongue of gules, ringed by five stars'. This description was incorrect, since there is no known example in heraldry of a star representing a province. In order to clear up this problem the Flemish Council approved the Olivier decree on 18th October 1990, which removed the stars from the coat of arms of the Flemish Community. The arms of the Flemish Community adorn the writing paper and envelopes of the Flemish Parliament.

national mandate, and would certainly not have been chosen voluntarily by certain members. The result of this was that, certainly in its early years, the Flemish parliament included members who were not in favour of the institution, and who tried to undermine its powers from within.

Achievements

Despite its weak institutional basis, the Flemish cultural parliament was able to present a not unfavourable final balance in 1980. A total of 49 decrees had been approved between 1971 and 1980. A number of these dealt with the use of language, and their objective was always the same: to curb the use of French in the Dutch language area and where possible to disallow it. The most important language decree was the Vandezande decree of 19th July 1973, which became familiar under the name *September Decree*. It laid down that from then on employers in Flanders were to speak Dutch in their contacts with their employees and that they were allowed to use only Dutch for all legally prescribed contracts and documents. It was only in September that the implications of the decree penetrated into the French-speaking part of the country. There then arose a campaign against 'le décret de septembre' in the French-speaking press, which ultimately resulted in an anti-Flemish smear campaign. The September Decree demonstrated that the Flemish cultural parliament really did have genuine power, even if it was in a limited number of areas.

In addition to the language decrees, a great many were approved whose aim was the democratization of Flemish cultural life. There were important decrees in the fields of adult education, youth-work, libraries, sport and open-air activities, all intended to facilitate greater participation by broad bands of the population in the cultural life. Among the series of democratization decrees, the *Library Decree* of 19th June 1978 deserves a special mention, since it obliged every Flemish municipality to establish a public library.

A third important area of activity of the cultural parliament was the protection of the Flemish cultural heritage, and more particularly the preservation of monuments. It is no exaggeration to say that the present policy on monuments was created by the culturally autonomous Flanders. The neglect of the Flemish cultural heritage, and of the Belgian cultural heritage in general, was probably one of the most striking characteristics of postwar national cultural policy.

In conclusion, as an extension of the language decrees, the Flemish cultural parliament approved another six decrees intended to bolster the reputation of the Dutch language.

In 1973 the Flemish cultural parliament organized an advertising campaign to promote its publications. At that time it was still extremely unusual for a public institution, and certainly a parliament, to recommend its publications to the public at large by way of the media.

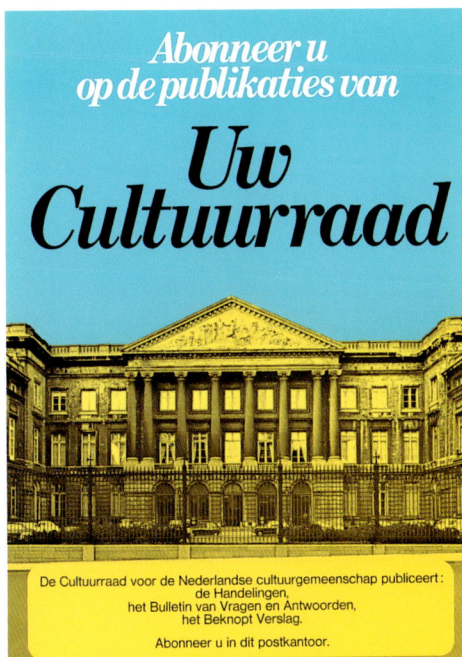

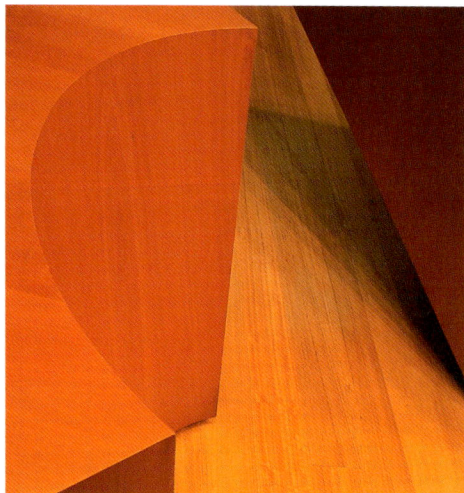

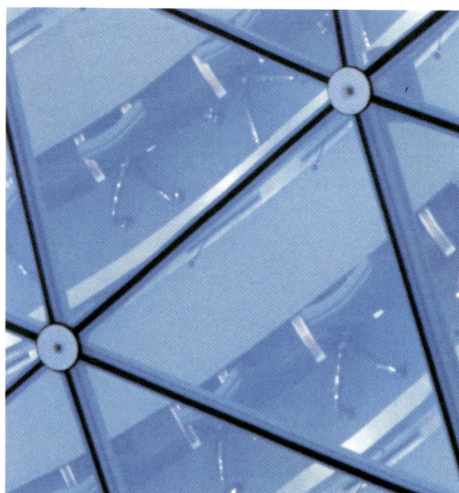

The overall positive balance obtained by the Flemish parliament, which compares favourably with the rather meagre achievements of the cultural parliament of the French cultural community, is explained mainly by the fact that the Flemish cultural parliament offered the Dutch Cultural Community the opportunity to do something about major historical complaints itself. This was true not only on the language issue. The pursuit of a cultural policy of its own had also been an important area of action for the Flemish Movement since the second half of the thirties.

Speakers

The Flemish cultural parliament assembled for the first time on Tuesday 7th December 1971, in the chamber of the lower house (Chamber of People's Representatives). The inaugural meeting was presided over by the VU senator Leo Elaut. During the meeting, the assembly appointed the CVP senator and party chairman Robert Vandekerckhove as its first Speaker. He was followed by Jan Bascour (PVV, 1974-1977), Maurits Coppieters (VU, 1977-1979) and Rik Boel (SP, 1979-1980) in the office of Speaker of the Flemish cultural parliament.

Seat

The Belgian legislators had made no provisions for the accommodation of the cultural parliaments in the 1970 constitutional revision. The Flemish cultural parliament deduced from this that it was able to choose its location itself.

On 7th March 1972 the Cultural Council of the Dutch Cultural Community opted to use the national parliament building. In concrete terms this meant that all plenary meetings of the cultural parliament took place in the chamber of the lower house, and that it could use the house's committee rooms for its committee meetings.

By choosing the Palace of the Nation, the Flemish cultural parliament was at the same time opting for *Brussels*. In 1972 this was not the obvious choice. As has already been mentioned, in the sixties and seventies Brussels had developed into one of the most divisive issues between the Flemish and the Walloons. Therefore, it was not so evident that the Flemish cultural parliament should establish itself there. Certain parties were of the opinion that the autonomous Flemish cultural parliament should not establish itself in the capital of unitary Belgian power, but in a 'pure' Flemish city, such as Mechelen. Those who favoured Brussels argued that the Flemish presence in Brussels was essential, in order to demonstrate that, as Lode Craeybeckx expressed it in 1954, 'Flanders would not let go of Brussels'.

In the end Brussels was chosen. This was to be a definitive choice: when the Flemish parliament decided to buy a building in the Belgian parliamentary district in 1987, there was not even a word of debate. At that time, the promotion of the presence of the Flemish authorities in Brussels, which the Flemish parliament had already proclaimed capital of Flanders in 1984, had become a major line of force in the policy of the politically autonomous Flanders.

Public image

The first parliament for the Flemish had to contend with an image problem throughout the seventies: the cultural parliament was little known among the Flemish people, and even fewer realized what its task and status was. The major cause of this unfamiliarity was undoubtedly the fact that the cultural parliament had neither the form nor the image of an independent parliament: its areas of competence were limited, its members were also members of the national parliament, it met in the rooms of the lower house and, what's more, its unfortunately selected official name – the Cultural Council – did not add to its prestige. These external features illustrated the fact that, despite its genuine legislative power, the Flemish cultural parliament remained embedded in the essentially unitary Belgian state structure, in which it necessarily played a subordinate part.

Despite this difficult point of departure, in the seventies the successive

Speakers and their Bureaus made notable efforts to make the parliament more widely known by means of targeted campaigns. In 1973 and 1978 booklets were published on the institution's areas of competence and operation, in 1973 a large-scale campaign was launched advertising the cultural parliament's publications, and in 1978 the celebration of the 11th of July was organized for the first time.

Between 1980 and 1996: from cultural parliament to full Flemish Parliament

THE CONSTITUTIONAL REVISIONS OF 1980, 1988 AND 1993

The *community conflicts* between the Flemish and the Walloons that flared up fiercely in the seventies proved that granting cultural autonomy to the cultural communities had definitely not entirely solved the tensions between them. If Belgium itself was to be saved, it was essential that Flanders and Wallony be given more autonomy, in other words a further transformation of the unitary state into a federal one was vital. In this situation Flanders was the party requesting an expansion of the cultural communities' areas of competence. Wallony pressed for the implementation of the formation of regions which had already been written into the Constitution in 1970.

The *1980 constitutional revision* was the Belgian parliament's decisive step towards the development of this federal state. This led to the birth in Belgium, alongside the central Belgian state, of politically autonomous *member states, communities and regions*, which were granted a far-reaching form of political self-rule.

On the one hand, the *communities* took over the authority of the former cultural communities, but in addition their authority was extended in the areas of health policy, care of the handicapped and youth policy. So in actual fact since 1980 there have existed in Belgium three 'communities' which have taken over a number of the areas of competence of the national state: the Flemish, French and German Communities. In 1980, Brussels was not made a separate community, just as in 1970 it had not become a separate cultural community.

The Flemish and French Communities each received their own legislative body – a parliament or *council* – and an executive body – the government.

Just like the Dutch Cultural Council, the Flemish
Council also met in the Lower House. From 1982
the Lion of Flanders graced the chamber when
there was a meeting.

These governments were elected by and from the community parliaments. In
other words, since 1980 the Flemish and French Communities have each had
their own parliamentary assembly *and* government. In this way, on the
Flemish side, the Flemish Community Parliament was born, officially entitled the *Flemish Community Council*, to succeed the Cultural Council for

The communities

The Flemish Community includes all the inhabitants of the Dutch language area as well as the Brussels Flemings, meaning the Dutch-speaking inhabitants of the bilingual Brussels Capital area. The French Community includes all the inhabitants of the French language area and the French-speaking inhabitants of Brussels. The German-speaking Community includes all the inhabitants of the German language area.

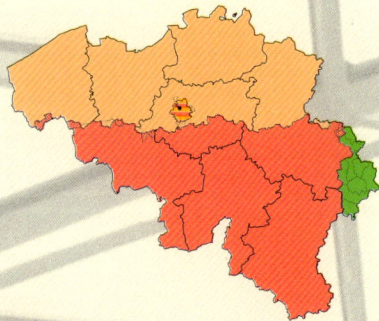

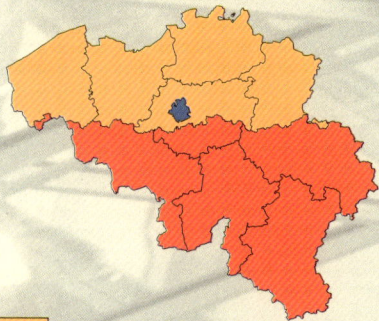

Flemish Community
French Community
Flemish and French Community
German Community

The regions

The Flemish Region covers the whole territory of the Dutch language area, the Walloon Region the territory of the French and German language areas, and the Brussels Capital Region the territory of the nineteen boroughs of the bilingual Brussels Capital area.
Brussels is a separate region, but not a separate community. The Brussels Flemings are part of the Flemish Community, the Brussels French-speakers of the French Community. Together they inhabit the Brussels Capital Region.

Flemish Region
Walloon Region
Brussels Capital Region

Merger of the Flemish Community and Flemish Region

In Flanders the community and the region were merged: Flanders has one Flemish Parliament and one Flemish Government. They have competence for both community and regional affairs.

Flanders
Brussels

The voting board above the Speaker's chair in the Domed Hall.

Perspective drawing of the Domed Hall, the hall for the plenary meetings of the Flemish Parliament.

▶

the Dutch Cultural Community. On the French side, the French Community Council succeeded the French Cultural Council. Like the former cultural councils, the Flemish and French Community Councils had authority over the monolingual Flemish and French-language institutions in Brussels.

In 1980 the formation of the regions was also implemented. At that time two regions were established, each with major areas of political competence – the Flemish Region and the Walloon Region. By contrast with the communities, which are political entities that in certain matters also have authority in Brussels, the regions are territorially defined areas whose authority is limited geographically to the boundaries of the region. *So, in contrast with the Flemish and French Communities, the Flemish and Walloon Regions did not have any power in Brussels.* The 1988 constitutional revision made Brussels into a third region with its own powers.

As Wallony had wanted, the regions were given authority in certain aspects of economic policy, but also in town and country planning, the environment and energy policy. Like the communities, the regions were given their own legislative body which could approve decrees with the power of law – a parliament or *council* – and an executive body – the government.

It was necessary to divide Belgium into two different sorts of member state, community and region because the Flemish and the Walloons have a different view of this federalization. For the Flemish the most important

motive was the pursuit of cultural autonomy for all Dutch speakers, including the Flemish people of Brussels. This aspiration formed the basis for the division of Belgium into three communities. Conversely, the Walloons were the party primarily requesting the ability to implement their own social and economic policy in the Walloon region, and attached less importance to their links with the French-speakers of Brussels. That's why they devoted most attention to the formation of the regions. In order to reach a compromise, two sorts of member state were ultimately established.

However, in 1980 Flanders made immediate use of the possibility of merging the community and the region. *In concrete terms this means that since 1980, there have on the Flemish side been one Flemish Parliament and one Flemish Government for both the Flemish Community and the Flemish Region.* In 'merging' the community and the region, Flanders wished to make clear that the Flemish people in Brussels were part of the Flemish Community and that Brussels could not become a separate third region like the other two. The term 'merge' should not be interpreted literally, however: the Flemish Region, with its geographical definition and its areas of competence, very definitely continued to exist after 1980. This was because the Flemish Community and the Flemish Region did not cover the same territory: the Flemish Community does have authority in Brussels, but the Flemish Region does not. This explains why, among other things, the Brussels Flemish do not have the vote on regional affairs in the Flemish parliament.

The consequences of the 1980 state reform for the Flemish parliament (officially called the *Flemish Council* since this state reform) can be summarized as follows:

First of all the Flemish Council was given considerably more areas of competence than its predecessor, the Dutch Cultural Council. This enabled it to make a greater mark on Flemish policy.

In addition to this, in 1980 the Flemish Council was granted a major new area of competence, characteristic of a full parliament, namely the right to appoint its own Flemish government. Politically, the Flemish government is answerable to the Flemish Parliament. This means it can be dismissed by the parliament if, according to the latter, it is not performing its task properly. The Flemish Parliament appointed a total of eight governments between 1980 and 1996: four were led by Gaston Geens (CVP) (1980-1992) and four by Luc Van den Brande (CVP) (1992-).

The *1988 constitutional revision* once more considerably expanded the Flemish Council's areas of competence to include the whole range of education and major sections of public works and transport. For this reason, under

From October 1976 to the end of 1997, the various departments of the Flemish Parliament were housed in the offices of the Ministry of Finance, adjacent to the Lower House. Despite the occupation of the Flemish Parliament building, the Flemish MPs have been housed in offices in the immediate vicinity of the Flemish Parliament building since 1996, and the departments of the Flemish Parliament since the end of 1997. This will continue until completion of the planned renovation of the former Postcheque head office has been completed, between the IJzerenkruisstraat and the Leuvenseweg.

the special finance law of 16th January 1989, the financial resources for Flanders' own policy-making body increased enormously: in 1980 the Flemish Parliament had a budgeted revenue of 40 billion BEF, in 1988 93 billion, in 1989 342 billion and in 1996 537 billion (nominal figures).

The great significance of the St. Michael's Agreement, concluded on 29th September 1992, which ultimately led to the *1993 constitutional revision*, is that it finally put an end to the double mandate system, whereby the members of the Flemish parliament were in the first place members of the Belgian upper and lower houses. Since the elections of 21st May 1995, the Flemish parliament has been an independent, directly elected body. This attainment formed the provisional endpiece to the transformation of the Belgian state from a unitary to a federal model.

The first directly elected Flemish Parliament was installed on 13th June 1995. It elected Norbert De Batselier (SP) to be its new Speaker. To conclude that meeting the Flemish Council changed its name to the *Flemish Parliament* and laid down that its members would from then on be called *Flemish People's Representatives* (MPs). These decisions were officially ratified on the eve of the opening of the Flemish Parliament building – 14th March 1996.

However, in addition to its direct election, the 1993 state reform gave the Flemish parliament another major instrument for its continued development: the *constitutive autonomy*. This meant that the parliament was itself able to change certain rules regarding its composition, election and operation. For example, it can change the number of its members, formulate additional items irreconcilable with the mandate of Flemish MP, and change the constituencies for the Flemish Parliament. On top of this, constitutive autonomy also provides far-reaching powers with regard to establishing the operation of the Flemish government. The Flemish Parliament can by this means itself create the framework within which the Flemish political landscape will develop in the twenty-first century.

THE PARLIAMENT FOR THE FLEMINGS, 1980-1996

Achievements

Between 1980 and 1996 the Flemish Parliament slowly but surely expanded into a full-fledged parliamentary assembly. This could in the first place be seen from the *numerous decrees* it approved in its various areas of competence – 313 between 1980 and 1995, and which gradually created a characteristic Flemish model of society. A number of typically Flemish institutions came into being, including the Vlaamse Dienst voor Arbeidsbemiddeling (VDAB) (Flemish Employment and Vocational Training Office), the Sociaal-Economische Raad voor Vlaanderen (SERV) (Social and Economic Council of Flanders), Kind en Gezin (Child and Family) and De Lijn (The Line – public

The Domed Hall

transport company). After 1980 the foundations were also laid, in most areas of competence, for a characteristically Flemish policy. We shall mention here only the Kabeldecreet (Cable Decree) of 28th January 1987, which smoothed the way for commercial television in Flanders, the waste-product, water, wood and dune decrees, which shaped Flanders' own environmental policy, the various education decrees that gave a definitively Flemish character to educational policy, and the decrees concerning administrative policy and openness of administration which laid the foundations for a new official culture.

In addition to the task of issuing decrees, the Flemish Parliament's *regulatory task* also reached full development between 1980 and 1996. In contrast to the period of the cultural parliament, when ministers who were members of the national government turned up for the Flemish Parliament, while not being politically responsible for it, after 1980 the Flemish Council was able to demand its own ministers, and abandon its confidence in an individual minister or in the government as a whole. This gave full significance to the *right of interpellation*, and the Flemish Parliament made use of it, with twin intentions: on the one hand to exercise effective control over the implementation and observance of the decrees passed, and on the other to check whether successive Flemish governments sufficiently promoted the community interests of Flanders in the Belgian federal state system. It was especially in the expansion of this second element that the growth of the parliament of the Flemish expressed itself in the 1980-1996 period. The number of interpellations and questions on the relationships between Flanders, Wallony and Brussels increased regularly. Examples include the Voeren situation and the debate on the financial transfers from Flanders to Wallony. So between 1980 and 1996

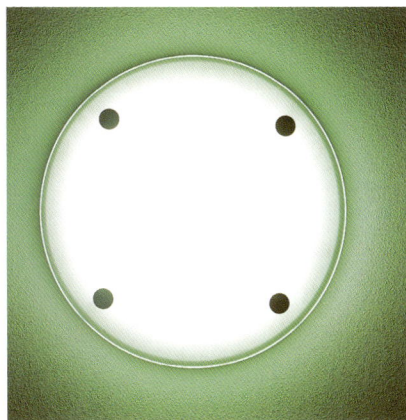

The Flemish Community in Brussels

In 1985 the Flemish Government decided to house its offices in the heart of Brussels. In 1989 they occupied the Marquis Building, in the immediate vicinity of St. Michael's Cathedral, followed in 1990 by the Baudouin Building, located at the northern gateway to the city of Brussels.

Since May 1993, the offices of the ministers of the Flemish government have been housed on or in the immediate surroundings of the historic Martyrs' Square in the centre of Brussels. Martyrs' Square lies on the same axis as the Marquis Building and the Baudouin Building. This 'Flemish axis' is symbolic of the lasting presence of the Flemish authorities in Brussels.

Left to right: Martyrs' Square, the Marquis Building, the Baudouin Building.

the Flemish Parliament grew into a new and important *political forum* in the Belgian community landscape.

Speakers

The Flemish Council met for the first time on 21st October 1980. During the meeting on 4th November 1980, Rik Boel, who had been the Speaker of the Flemish cultural parliament since 24th April 1979, was confirmed in his office. After him the successive Speakers of the Flemish Council were Jean Pede (PVV, 1981-1985), Frans Grootjans (PVV, 1985-1988), Jean Pede (PVV, Feb 1988 - Oct 1988), Louis Vanvelthoven (SP, 1988-1994) and Eddy Baldewijns (SP, 1994-1995). On 13th June 1995 Norbert De Batselier (SP) became the speaker of the first directly elected Flemish parliament, which has since that very day officially been known as the Flemish Parliament.

Seat

Like the Cultural Council of the Dutch Cultural Community, from 1980 the Flemish Council met in the chambers of the lower house. As the Flemish Council increasingly assumed the appearance of a full parliament, the need to acquire its own building also grew.

As early as 1983 the Bureau – the executive committee – had had its eye on the former *Hôtel des Postes et de la Marine* in Brussels' neutral zone. On 21st October 1986 it was announced that the national government wished, in exchange for a symbolic franc, to hand over the desired building, situated on the corner of the Leuvenseweg and the Hertogstraat, to the Flemish Community, which then in its turn passed it on to the Flemish Council on 5th May 1987. After a difficult process of building and conversion, which took much longer than originally planned, the *Flemish Parliament building* was brought into use early in 1996.

As noted above, in 1987 the choice of Brussels was no longer under discussion. By that time the Flemish presence in Brussels had already become the most natural thing. One of the reasons for the Flemish Community and the Flemish Region merging in 1980 was the concern to demonstrate that Brussels really was part of Flanders; the decree issued on 6th March 1984 proclaimed Brussels capital of the Flemish Community; the Flemish administrative departments and the offices of the Flemish government were established in the heart of Brussels. The selection of Brussels for the seat of the Flemish Parliament forms an integral part of this policy of presence.

Public image
The Flemish Council also had an image problem to contend with, just like the cultural parliament. Regarded purely rationally, this obscurity was hard to explain: the Flemish Council's areas of competence systematically increased between 1980 and 1995, substantial and innovative work was done, the Flemish Council increasingly let its voice be heard when Flemish interests were threatened by the national state, the French Community or the Walloon Region, and after 1988 the press devoted markedly more attention to the activities of the Flemish Council.

But, like the Cultural Council in the preceding period, the Flemish Council suffered constantly from a great many handicaps that meant its significance often eluded the public. The double mandate and its accommodation in the national parliament building hindered the creation of an identity separate from that of the national parliament. At the same time the unfortunately chosen official name did not point directly to a parliamentary assembly. What's more, the Flemish Council was often eclipsed by the Flemish government, which was more successful in acquiring a recognizable identity of its own.

After 1988, a greater attempt was made to increase the public's familiarity with the name, by organizing numerous public relations activities, including the colloquium on 'Dutch in the World', the public-speaking competition for pupils of the two last years of secondary education, the annual 11th of July celebrations and the annual presentation of honorary awards to deserving Flemings. Even then, on the eve of the first direct election to the Flemish Parliament, this familiarity did not come up to expectations.

There are for the moment still no objective data regarding this question, but one may assume that familiarity with the name of the Flemish Parliament has increased in the last year. The first direct election undoubtedly increased many Flemings' knowledge of the new institutions. Three important initiatives the institution itself has recently undertaken, have contributed to this: the change of name from Flemish Council to Flemish Parliament, the occupation of the Flemish Parliament building, and, most especially, the guided tours of this building.

A historical shot: the first 124 directly elected
Flemish MPs, photographed on the occasion of
the official opening of the Flemish Parliament
building on Sunday 17th March 1996.

Group photo of
the Flemish MPs

1. Johan De Roo
2. Veerle Heeren
3. Ria Van Den Heuvel
4. Trees Merckx - Van Goey
5. Vera Dua
6. Stefaan Platteau
7. Filip Dewinter
8. Paul Van Grembergen
9. André Denys
10. Ward Beysen
11. Georges Cardoen
12. Marc Olivier
13. Norbert De Batselier
14. Francis Vermeiren
15. Kathy Lindekens
16. Marleen Vanderpoorten
17. Maria Tyberghien - Vandenbussche
18. Patricia Ceysens
19. Mia De Schamphelaere

20. Yolande Avontroodt
21. Gracienne Van Nieuwenborgh
22. Jean-Marie Bogaert
23. Herman Suykerbuyk
24. Michel Doomst
25. Brigitte Grouwels
26. Michiel Vandenbussche
27. Jos Geysels
28. Louis Bril
29. Jaak Gabriels
30. Johan Malcorps
31. Jacques Laverge
32. Cecile Verwimp - Sillis
33. Arnold Van Aperen
34. Mandus Verlinden
35. Georges Beerden
36. Johan Weyts
37. Nelly Maes
38. Freddy Feytons
39. Frans Wymeersch
40. Pieter Huybrechts
41. Frank Creyelman
42. Jan Caubergs

43. Lydia Maximus
44. André Kenzeler
45. Johan Sauwens
46. Jozef Browaeys
47. Anny De Maght - Aelbrecht
48. Herman Candries
49. Jacques Devolder
50. Marcel Logist
51. Herman De Loor
52. Carl Decaluwé
53. Marino Keulen
54. Freddy De Vilder
55. Erik Matthijs
56. Marijke Dillen
57. Roland Deswaene
58. Sonja Becq
59. Riet Van Cleuvenbergen
60. Etienne Van Vaerenbergh
61. Jef Van Looy
62. Leo Cannaerts
63. Eddy Schuermans
64. Patrick Lachaert
65. René Swinnen

66. Jacky Maes
67. Guy Swennen
68. Peter De Ridder
69. Hugo Marsoul
70. Christian Verougstraete
71. Mark Van der Poorten
72. Jacques Timmermans
73. John Taylor
74. Dirk Van Mechelen
75. Leo Goovaerts
76. Peter Vanvelthoven
77. Didier Ramoudt
78. Julien Demeulenaere
79. Paul Dumez
80. Freddy Sarens
81. Gilbert Vanleenhove
82. Marc Cordeel
83. Leonard Quintelier
84. Mieke Van Hecke
85. Bruno Tobback
86. Steve Stevaert
87. Robert Voorhamme
88. Kris Van Dijck
89. Roeland Van Walleghem
90. Dominiek Lootens - Stael
91. Emiel Verrijken
92. Jos De Meyer
93. Patrick Hostekint
94. Paul Deprez
95. Leo Delcroix
96. Marc Van Peel
97. Karel De Gucht
98. Herman De Reuse
99. Karim Van Overmeire
100. Jan Penris
101. Felix Strackx
102. Joris Van Hauthem
103. Peter Desmet
104. Willy Kuijpers
105. Bart Vandendriessche
106. Jos Stassen
107. Walter Vandenbossche
108. Ludo Sannen
109. Jef Sleeckx
110. André Van Nieuwkerke
111. Herman Lauwers
112. Tuur Van Wallendael
113. Chris Vandenbroeke
114. Gilbert Bossuyt
115. Sonja Van Lindt
116. Fred Dielens

117. Etienne De Groot
118. Johnny Goos
119. Wilfried Aers
120. Luk Van Nieuwenhuysen
121. Joachim Coens
122. Carlos Lisabeth
123. Hugo Van Rompaey
124. Gaston Denayer - Secretary General

Absent from the photo: Christian Van Eyken

Group photo of the Flemish ministers and Flemish MPs

1. Luc Martens
2. Eric Van Rompuy
3. Eddy Baldewijns
4. Luc Van den Bossche
5. Luc Van den Brande
6. Theo Kelchtermans
7. Wivina Demeester - De Meyer
8. Leo Peeters
9. Anne Van Asbroeck

2
Historical outline of the Flemish Parliament building

At the end of the eighteenth century, the stately Edel-Concert building rose on the site where the Flemish Parliament building now stands. This was the rendezvous for sophisticated Brussels. After Belgium's independence in 1830, the former concert hall served as, among other things, a Freemasons' lodge, until it was compulsorily purchased in 1874. The Edel-Concert was demolished at the end of the nineteenth century and the resulting space was integrated into the architectural concept of the ministry district which had been under construction in the neighbourhood of the Palace of the Nation since the third quarter of the nineteenth century. On this site, at the corner of the Leuvenseweg and the Hertogstraat, rose the 'Hôtel des Postes et de la Marine'. This accommodated the offices of the executive committee of the Post Office and the Office of Marine Affairs and at a later date those of the Postcheque Service too. The Flemish Council bought the building in 1987.

The Edel-Concert, a building of style (1779-1895)

THE CONSTRUCTION OF THE WARANDE DISTRICT AT THE END OF THE AUSTRIAN PERIOD, 1770-1795

Although it is hard to imagine, the concentration of people and traffic that today characterizes the area round the Wetstraat in Brussels, the political heart of Belgium, is a relatively recent phenomenon. This neighbourhood was until the second half of the eighteenth century an oasis of peace and quiet. It formed part of the *warande* (pleasure park) of the Dukes of Brabant, whose palace was on the higher ground of the Koudenberg. From the palace at the top of the Koudenberg hill a luxuriant rolling landscape of gardens and shrubs, embellished by a lake, stretched out northwards to the Leuvenseweg. The Dukes' Orangery had been built here too.

In 1731 the palace of the Dukes of Brabant was devastated by a raging fire. The governors serving the Habsburg Empress Maria Theresia found new accommodation in the nearby Hof van Nassau. This brought a sudden uncertainty to the future of the old palace and its wild pleasure park.

In 1770 it was decided not to rebuild the medieval palace. The whole area round the Koudenberg was to be laid out anew in the French Neo-classical style. The result was one of the most remarkable urban planning achievements of the eighteenth century: the Koningsplein and the adjoining new pleasure park.

The new park, today's Royal Park (also known as the Brussels Park or Warande Park) was transformed into a geometric park, with the perfect symmetry entirely in keeping with the Neo-classical style. The fanciful, unordered character of the old pleasure park was lost completely. Four new streets were laid round the new park – the Wetstraat, Hertogstraat, Koningstraat and Paleizenplein. Private individuals built a row of stately mansions or *hôtels* on the plots along the outer sides of the four streets in accordance with plans laid down by the authorities. In this way the Warande District became an area of classically inspired buildings linked by line and style to the Koningsplein and thereby creating unity of urban design. Since the rules of uniformity and symmetry were less than strictly adhered to – less imposing façades were allowed in the Hertogstraat in particular – and the greenery of the park provided a pleasant interruption of the architectural set-

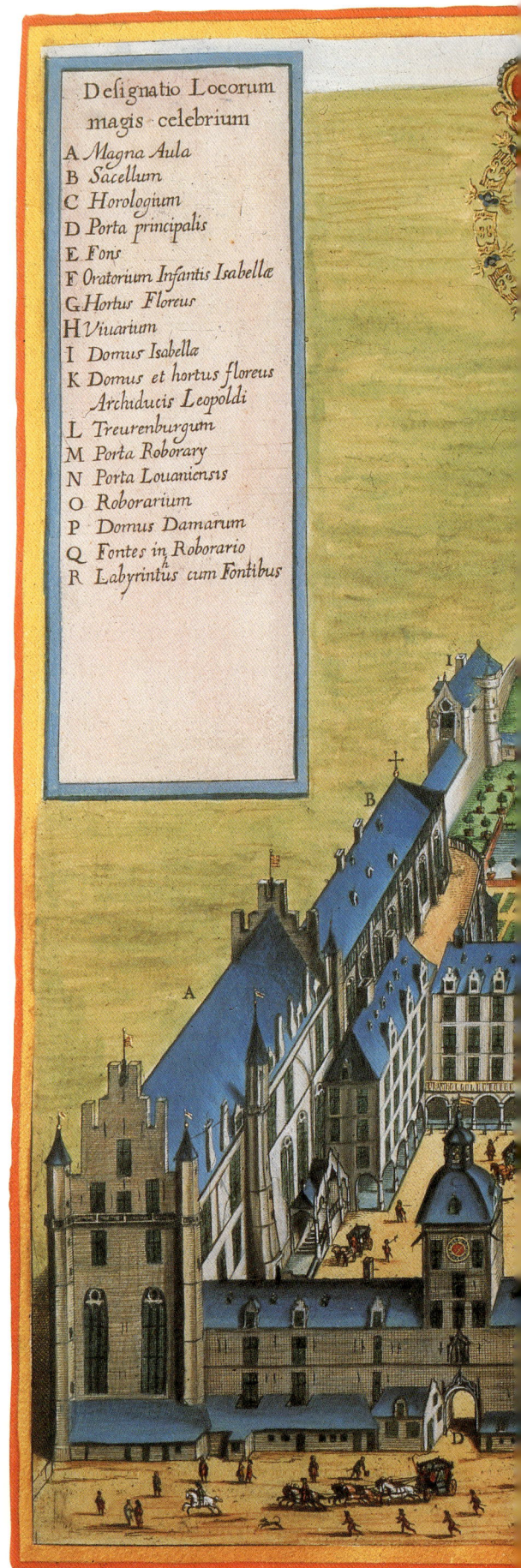

Designatio Locorum magis celebrium
A Magna Aula
B Sacellum
C Horologium
D Porta principalis
E Fons
F Oratorium Infantis Isabellæ
G Hortus Floreus
H Vivarium
I Domus Isabella
K Domus et hortus floreus Archiducis Leopoldi
L Treurenburgum
M Porta Roborary
N Porta Louaniensis
O Roborarium
P Domus Damarum
Q Fontes in Roborario
R Labyrintus cum Fontibus

ALATIVM BRVXELLENSE DVCIS BRABANTIÆ

PHILIPPO IIII
HISPANIARVM ET INDIARVM
REGI POTENTISSIMO
BRABANTIÆ DVCI
HANC PALATII BRVXELLENSIS
IMAGINEM A SE FACTAM
HONORIS AC VENERATIONIS ERGO
D D
LVCAS VORSTERMANS IVNIOR

Lucas Vorstermans Iunior schulpsit Aqua forti

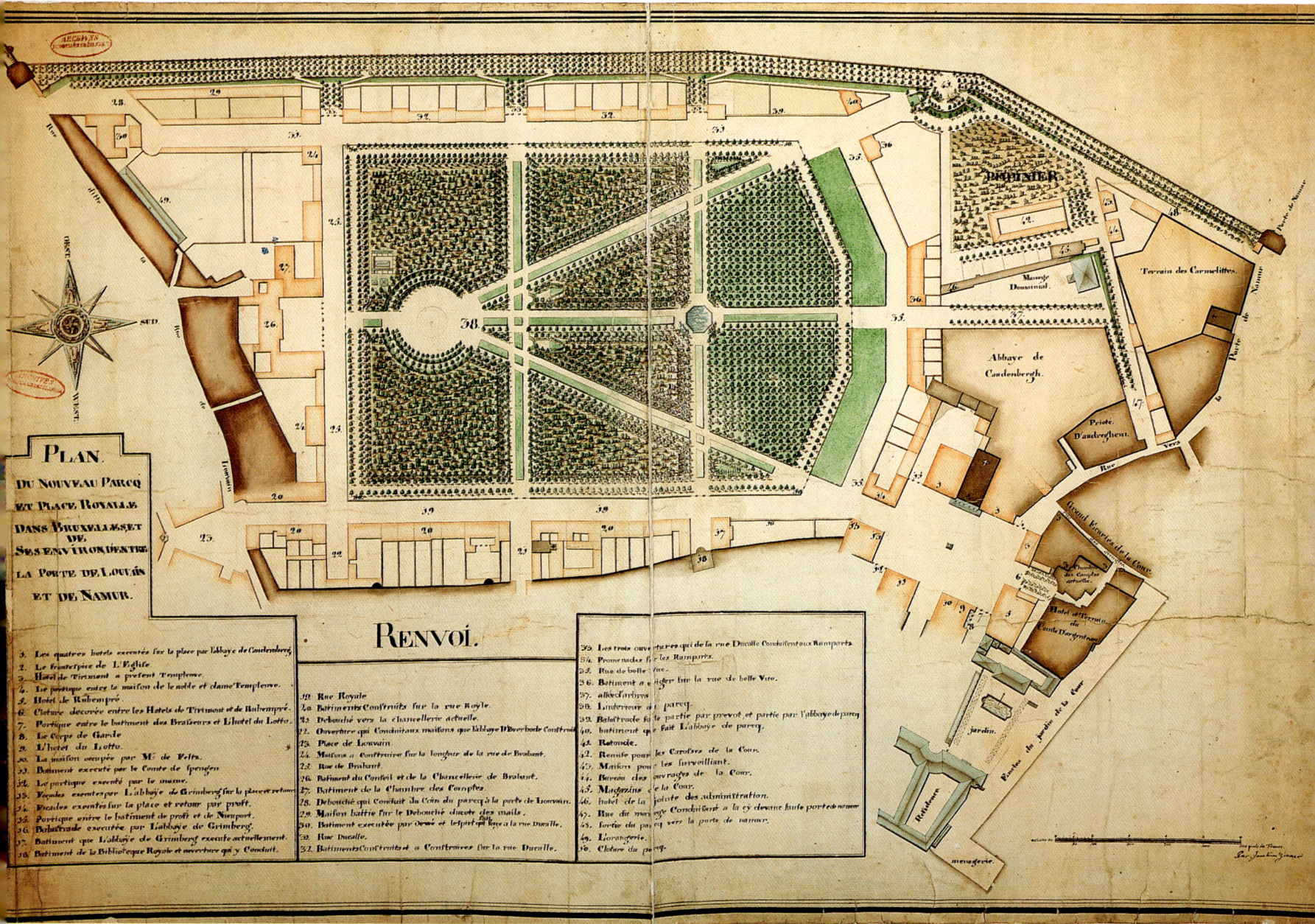

ting, there was no possibility of monotony. The Warande District became a captivating and exceptionally airy looking example of urban design in the Louis XVI style. The crowning glory was the monumental building for the Council of Brabant, now the Palace of the Nation, whose colonnade and fronton dominated the view.

Plan of the Brussels Park after the rebuilding of the Warande and the surrounding streets in the classicistic style (1779).

The palace of the Dukes of Brabant on the Koudenberg, the gardens and the 'warande' or pleasure park, at the peak of their growth (1659).

◄

A SPECIMEN OF THE CLASSICISTIC STYLE: DEWEZ' EDEL-CONCERT

It was in this context that in 1779 the architect Laurent-Benoit Dewez acquired a spacious plot of land on the corner of the Hertogstraat and the Leuvenseweg. This plot was on a spot where the Hertogstraat bends towards the Leuvensepoort: the current location of the Flemish Parliament building.

In 1760, after his studies and numerous study trips abroad, Dewez (1731-1812) came to live in Brussels. His chief involvement was in the building of major abbeys such as Affligem, Orval, Ninove and Vlierbeek, as well as the castles at Seneffe and Tervuren. In 1767 he became the court architect to the governor Charles of Lorraine. Dewez promoted the Louis XVI style in the Southern Netherlands.

The building Dewez planned for the corner of the Hertogstraat and the Leuvenseweg was within the new Warande District and had to comply with the strict architectural specifications imposed by its designers on the surrounding streets. Dewez' plans were for a ballroom and concert hall, which he would then let to the *Société de l'Académie de la Musique*, which at the end of the eighteenth century was one of the most important musical associations in Brussels. In fact the Société was closely involved in planning the new concert hall.

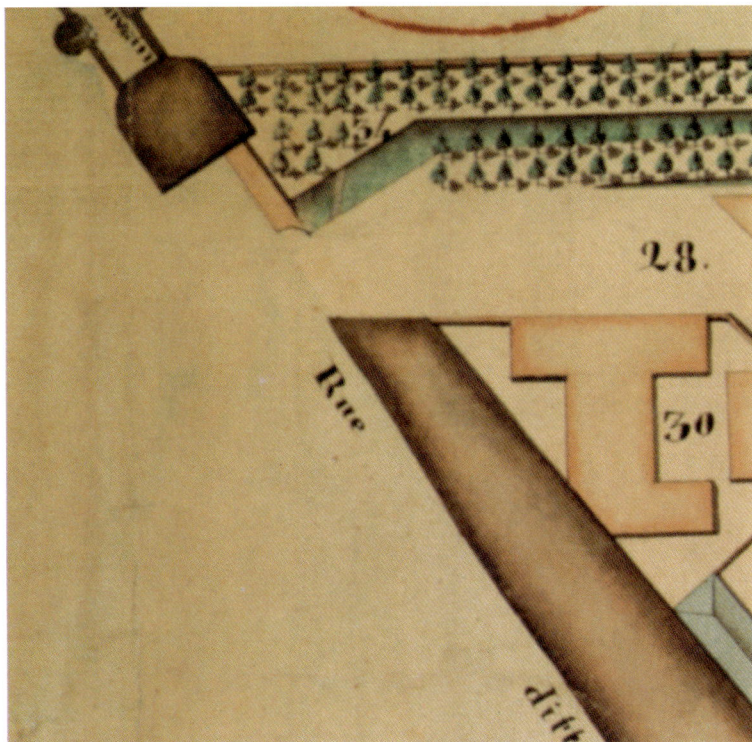

The 'Bâtiment exécutée par Dewé et lesprit qui fait face à la rue Ducalle' is number 30.

At about the same time another place of entertainment, the so-called *Waux-Hall*, came into being in the Warande Park, whose theatre is now known as the Royal Park Theatre.

The building Dewez designed for the Société fitted in perfectly with the architecture of the new Warande District and did full justice to its sophisticated style. The facade of the front part of the building, with its colossal pilasters, fronton, balustrade and urns closed off the view down the Hertogstraat. Behind this front section there was an open courtyard, behind which rose a second building. The plans that have been preserved have all the appearance of its being an impressive complex.

Dewez' complex of rooms became known as the *Edel-Concert* or *Concert-Noble*, after the noble *Société du Concert Noble* association, which operated under the auspices of the Société de l'Académie de la Musique, and was the building's main user. In fact in

52

1779 the part of the Hertogstraat between the present Wetstraat and the Leuvensepoort was renamed the *Edel-Concert straet* or *rue du Concert-Noble*. So the building was known not only under its French name, but also the Dutch. This was by no means usual in eighteenth-century Brussels, where the French influence was extremely strong. One more thing that should be said is that between 1786 and 1790, and again from 1802 to 1803, the Edel-Concert was also used by *Les Vrais Amis de l'Union*, a Freemasons lodge.

One of Dewez' designs for an interior gives us a better idea of the decoration of one of the Edel-Concert rooms. One wall had three double doors and two semicircular mirrors. Between the doors and the mirrors there were narrow panels showing trophies in bas-relief. Rectangular panels above the doors and mirrors contained sculptured allegories of art and music. Freestanding columns were planned in both corners. A second short wall had two double doors. Between them was a semicircular recess flanked by two fluted freestanding columns. The recess was to contain a monumental circular porcelain stove with heraldic symbols of the Habsburgs on its crown. Busts in relief appeared above the doors. A third, equally short wall comprised three horizontal sections. Mirrors or windows were worked into the lowermost. Above this the drawing shows three boxes enclosed by a balustrade. Two fluted freestanding columns were drawn in the corners. On the ceiling was a large semicircular corner moulding. The room was decorated in an exceptionally refined Louis XVI style. This was probably the ballroom and the boxes with balustrades were reserved for the musicians. The architect Hendrik Beyaert used the principle of keeping the musicians out of sight a hundred years later in the large Concert Noble ballroom in the Aarlenstraat.

The governor gave a ball in the Edel-Concert rooms every year. All the members of the Société du Concert Noble then had the opportunity to meet the archdukes personally. This enabled the lower nobility, who did not have access to the court, to come close to the archdukes.

The grand façade of the old Edel-Concert, designed by Dewez (1779). This façade closed off the view down the Hertogstraat.

When the French revolutionaries had definitively beaten the Austrian army in 1795, and the Austrian Netherlands came under French rule, the Edel-Concert was for a time put to a different use. The French revolutionary laws regarding the abolition of the nobility also applied to the Belgian provinces, and in 1794 the Société du Concert Noble was, as a noble association, officially forbidden. Dewez' complex of rooms was put to new use as the *Tribunal Criminel*.

In 1798 Dewez sold the Edel-Concert to the concertmaster Jean-Joseph Pauwels, who from then on ran the rooms under the name *Grand Concert*. Now it was the middle-class musical associations that organized the concerts.

The first major performance in the Grand Concert took place in 1801. Under the baton of 'citoyen' Pauwels, Parisian musicians gave a concert that included a symphony by Haydn. On 29th July 1803, the First Consul, Napoleon, and his consort Joséphine de Beauharnais visited Brussels. On that occasion the couple were given a festive reception and a concert in the Grand Concert. They dismounted from their carriages to musical accompaniment.

The guests were taken to the large reception room, where Bonaparte was given the place of honour. The room was decorated with a thousand candles which were reflected by the numerous mirrors.

When, after the recognition of an imperial nobility in 1805, the Société de l'Académie de la Musique was allowed to operate once more, the former Edel-Concert was still let to Pauwels, and the Société could not put on all its concerts there. Even so, the association was closely involved in the organization of concerts in its former hall. The Brussels Conservatory also made regular use of the Grand Concert.

The Grand Concert remained one of the attractions of sophisticated Brussels during the Kingdom of the Netherlands period too. On 7th February 1815 a masked ball was held in honour of the Prince of Orange. On 5th March 1815 the Crown Prince was regaled with a magnificent dinner at the Grand Concert, to which 175 guests were invited. A giant portrait of William I hung in the room, draped in all the colours of the allied monarchies. The ball started at nine o'clock and created an atmosphere reminiscent of the splendour at the end of the eighteenth century.

In 1818 the Société de l'Académie de la Musique started negotiations with Pauwels to hire its former permanent concert hall for a longer period once again. The discussions were fruitless, however. At this, the association decided to move permanently into new reception rooms in the Waux-Hall, which was at that time called the Cercle Gaulois. The rental contract expired in 1874 and then the Société, which had changed its name to *Société Concert Noble* shortly after Belgian independence, moved into the monumental Concert Noble in the Aarlenstraat, designed by Hendrik Beyaert.

The history of the Edel-Concert after 1830 is less clear. The building probably fell into disuse, until part of it was bought by the *Les Amis Philanthropes* Freemasons lodge in 1869. Though ceremonially opened in 1869, an initial 'small' temple only came into use in 1870. The 'large' temple that had been planned never appeared. It is not known what the decoration of the small temple, done to a design by the architect Wijnand Janssens (1827-1913), looked like, nor his designs for the decoration of the large temple, which were of course never carried out.

In 1874 a compulsory purchase order made to enable the extension of the ministry district round the Palace of the Nation sealed the fate of Dewez' complex of rooms, in which various ministerial offices were housed until it was demolished about twenty years later.

The Hôtel des Postes et de la Marine, a monumental ministry (1895-1987)

THE CREATION OF THE MINISTRY DISTRICT ROUND THE PALACE OF THE NATION, 1830-1900

With the occupation of the former Council of Brabant building by the States General of the Netherlands between 1815 and 1830, and by the Belgian parliament after 1830, there was a considerable change to the appearance of the sophisticated district round the Warande Park, as it had developed since the late Austrian period. New ministries had started to establish themselves in

After 1830 the surroundings of the Palace of the Nation expanded into a ministry district. The first ministry building, for Justice and Finance, dates from 1861-64. The Hôtel Engler in the Wetstraat was extended in perfect symmetry to achieve this. This is now the office of the federal Prime Minister, also known as 'no. 16 Wetstraat'.

The buildings of the Belgian Law Gazette (r) and the head office of Bridges and Roads (l), designed in 1876 and 1880, reflect the square of honour at the rear of the Palace of the Nation.

the immediate surroundings of the Palace of the Nation as early as the 1815-1830 period, and by 1847 the whole Wetstraat block was owned by the Belgian state. The various mansions – *hôtels* – with their annexes provided accommodation for the ministers' official residences and administrative offices.

In the second half of the nineteenth century a start was made on the construction of a specific architectural heritage, adapted to the needs of the increasing number of ministries with an ever larger number of civil servants.

The first project of any size was a complex for the Ministries of Justice and Finance, which were completed between 1861 and 1864. To achieve this, a spacious office complex was added to the *Hôtel Engler*, the former refuge of the St Gertrude Abbey in Leuven, on the corner of the Wetstraat and the Hertogstraat, and now the office of the federal Prime Minister. This building was on the corner of the former Orangeriestraat, now the Hendrik Beyaert Binnenhof, which forms part of the Palace of the Nation. Two elongated wings linked it to the *Hôtel Walckiers*, the official residence of the Minister of Finance since 1836. The Hôtel Engler was also connected to the rear of the Palace of the Nation. Uniform plastered façades appear in both the Hertogstraat and the former Orangeriestraat, which were in total harmony with the architecture of the Wetstraat, in both measurements and prospect.

A second complex, intended for the Ministries of Home Affairs and War, was part of an all-embracing plan for new construction on the south side of the Leuvenseweg. Its main element was the expansion of the Palace of the Nation. The work was carried out between 1872 and 1879. The new buildings stretched from the newly laid-out Senate square on the Leuvenseweg to the corner of the Koningsstraat, behind the *Hôtel Torrington* and the *Hôtel des Galles*, which had been the official residences of the relevant ministers since 1834 and 1838 respectively. Here too the continuous facade was designed as a repetition of the façades along the Wetstraat. During the same period two symmetrical buildings were erected, occupying almost the entire length of the street, on the corner of the Leuvenseweg and the Parlementstraat, echoing the wings of the newly laid-out square at the Palace of the Nation. The architecture of these buildings, which were intended for the offices of the Belgian Law Gazette and for the executive board of Bridges and Roads and Mining, was also part of the overall plan for the new ministry district.

The provisional endpiece, and at the same time most extensive project in the development of the ministry district, was to be the block between the Leuvenseweg, the Hertogstraat and what is now the Hendrik Beyaert Binnenhof, traversed by the newly-planned Drukpersstraat. The sites involved, including the former Grand Concert, came under compulsory purchase in 1874. This project developed rapidly after the establishment of the Ministry of Railways, Post and Telegraph in 1884, which was to be housed there.

In an initial design drawn up by Goovaerts, the Chief Architect at the Department of Civil Buildings, there were two buildings for the new ministry. The design for the larger of the two, on the site of what is now the House of the Members of the Federal Parliament, was divided internally into seven small courtyards. The smaller building, where today's Flemish Parliament building stands, on the corner of the Leuvenseweg and the Hertogstraat, was seen as a rotunda, apparently intended to form a monumental symbol for the entrance to the district from the Leuvensepoort side. Goovaerts' plans were never carried out, however.

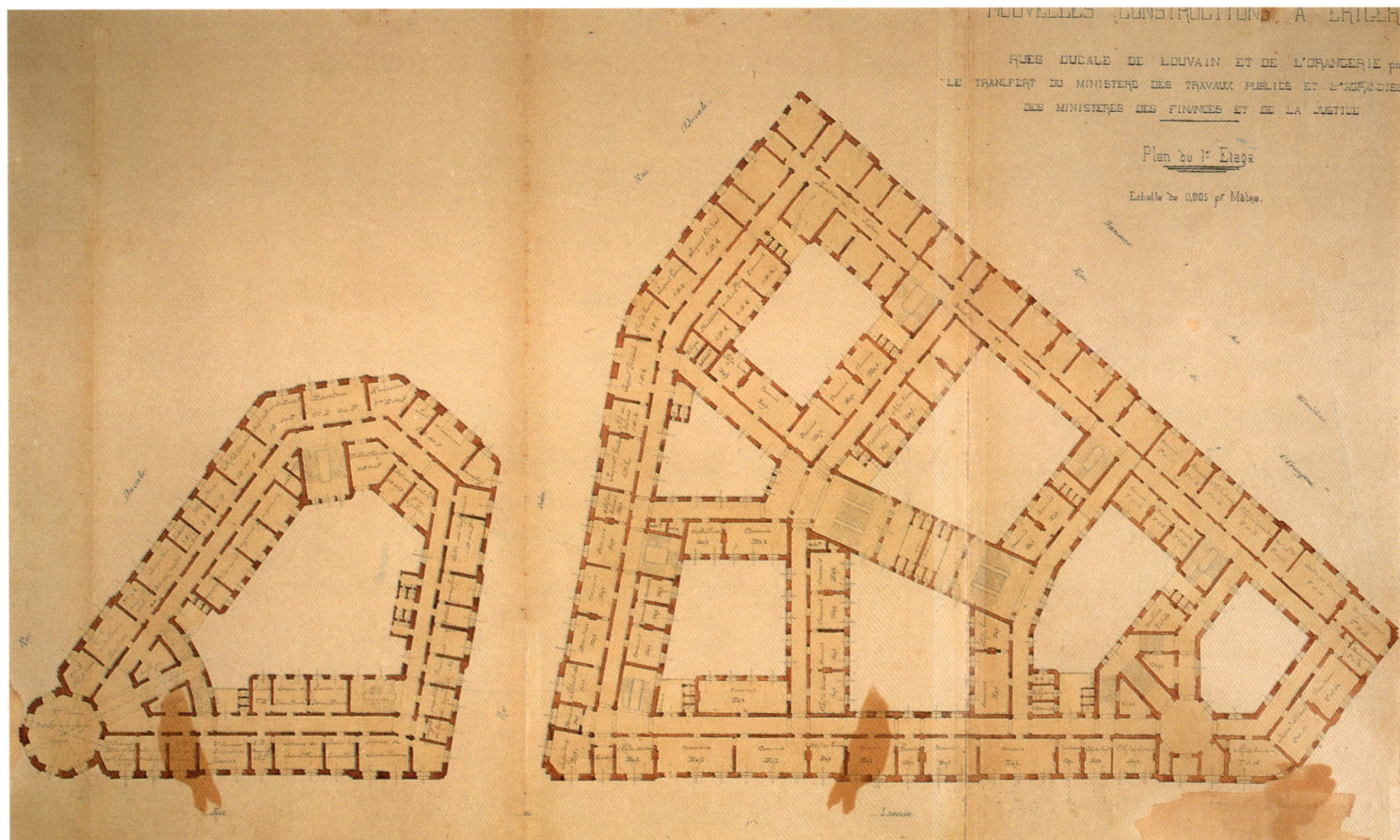

The endpiece of the 'ministry district' as designed by Goovaerts, the Chief Architect of Civil Buildings.

BEYAERT'S DESIGN FOR THE MINISTRY OF RAILWAYS, POST AND TELEGRAPH, 1886

In 1886 the architect Hendrik Beyaert was commissioned to draw up plans for the new buildings for the Ministry of Railways, Post and Telegraph, and the Office of Marine Affairs.

Beyaert (1823-1894) built up his career in the second half of the nineteenth century, serving the government, the nobility and the middle classes. He was born in Kortrijk and studied architecture at the academies of Kortrijk and Brussels. He started his career in 1851 by building a house in the Kunstlaan in Brussels, and the first casino-kursaal in Ostend. In 1859 he won the competition organized for the establishment of a new seat for the National Bank in Brussels. Beyaert's best-known creations include the National Bank buildings in Brussels and Antwerp, the ASLK (a bank) in the Wolvengracht in Brussels, the Hallepoort in Brussels and the already mentioned Concert Noble in the Aarlenstraat. Beyaert became best known as a promoter of the *Eclectic*

TRAVAUX D'ARCHITECTURE PAR H⁹ BEYAERT.

Pl. 1.

MINISTÈRE DES CHEMINS DE FER

A BRUXELLES

PLAN GÉNÉRAL DU REZ-DE-CHAUSSÉE

LÉGENDE

A Rez-de-chaussée et 2ᵐᵉ Étage: Voies
et Travaux.
1ᵉ Étage: Service général et Adminis-
trateurs.
B Les trois étages pour l'Exploitation.
C Les trois étages pour la Recette.
N.B. La division des bureaux, faite
en cloisons, est susceptible de chan-
gements selon les besoins du service.

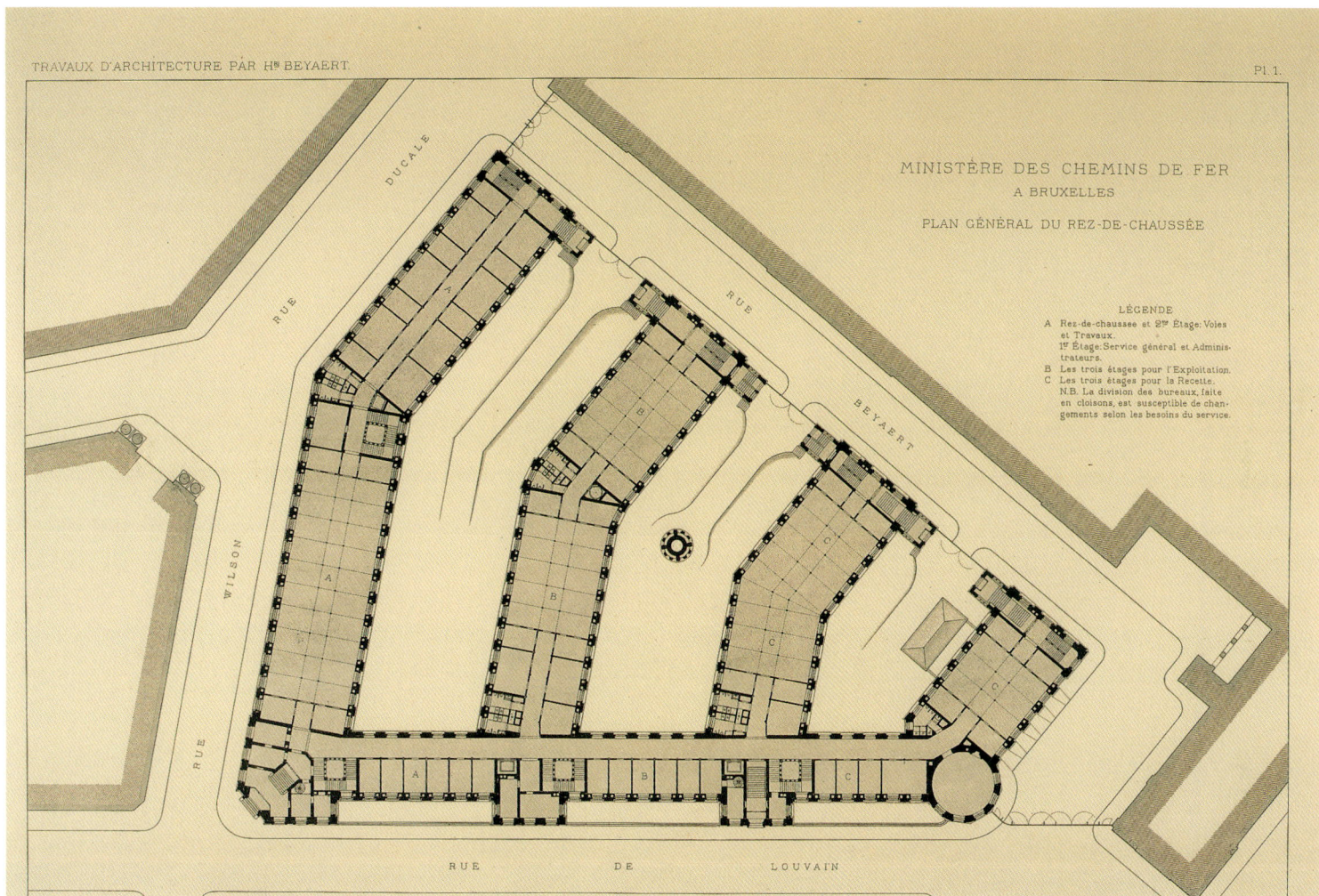

The plan of the Ministry of Railways is character-
ized by a succession of angled inner yards and a
flexible division of rooms.

The Ministry of Railways, to a design by Beyaert.
The contemporary 'classical' architecture with its
use of multicoloured materials contrasts with the
imitative Neo-classicism of the former ministry
buildings.

◄

Style. This style comprises the virtuoso combination of styles from the past
in which the designer aspires to a new, original style. His work, whose max-
ims were the pursuit of contemporary architecture and a dialogue with urban
space, forms an important link between Neo-classicism and Art Nouveau.

The first phase of the realization of Beyaert's design for the Ministry of
Railways, Post and Telegraph and the Office of Marine Affairs, was the construction of the Railways building, starting in 1889, which today is the House
of the Members of the federal Parliament. The closed character of Goovaerts'
design was replaced by airy angled inner yards oriented to the south, with the
still extant round tower in the axis of the Leuvenseweg as an identification
point. This kind of tower was characteristic of Beyaert's work, and can also be
seen in the buildings of the National Bank and the Hallepoort in Brussels.

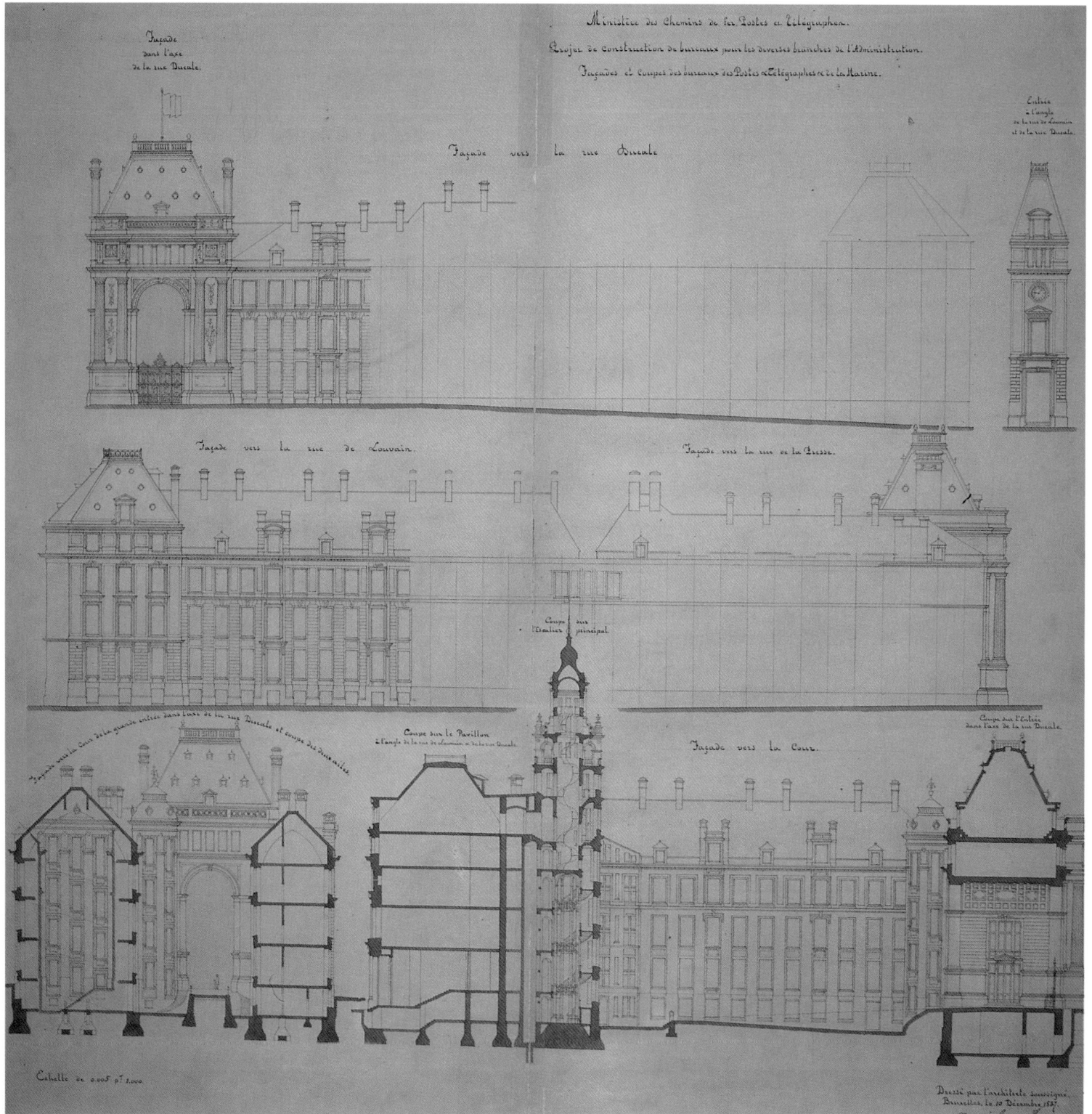

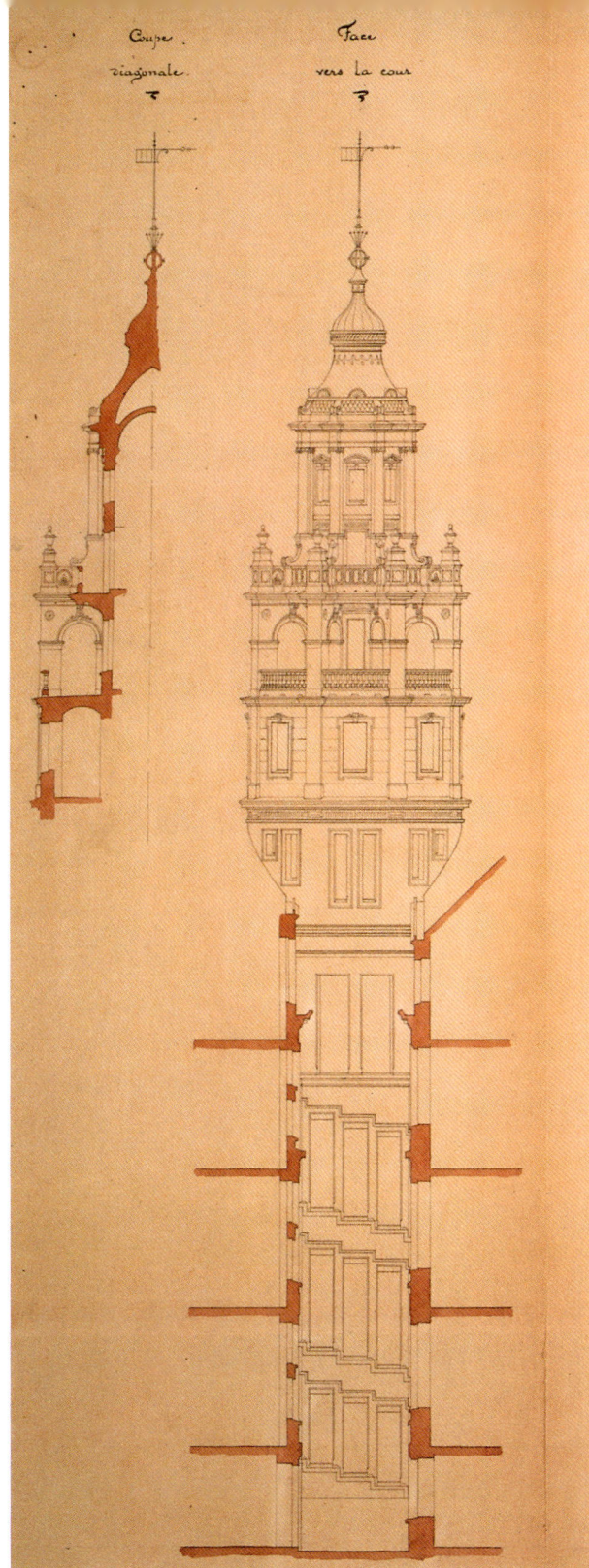

Coupe
diagonale.

Face
vers la cour

Beyaert's original design for the building for the Post Office and the Office of Marine Affairs. Detail of the façade of the staircase tower.

▶

Beyaert's original design for the building for the Post Office and the Office of Marine Affairs (1886), a rational counterpart to the Railways building. This building was marked by a triumphal arch and a staircase tower.

◀

In the second phase, the building for the Post and Marine Affairs on the site of what is now the Flemish Parliament building, Beyaert planned a sort of open triumphal arch on the corner of the Hertogstraat and the Drukpersstraat, in contrast to the closed grand façade of Dewez' Edel-Concert. The Hertogstraat was prolonged by a large irregular inner court and ended up at a cylindrical stair tower, the logical counterpart to the corner tower in the Railways building. Four wings enclosed an irregular diamond shape determined by the course of the surrounding streets. But after Beyaert died in 1894, this daring concept was not carried out.

The stair tower Beyaert had planned for the Post building but which was not built, would according to specialists have been one of his most refined creations in the genre: a cylindrical form, around which a spiral staircase would unfold, as in the National Bank and the Hallepoort in Brussels. And yet for the Post building Beyaert employed proportions which, particularly in connection with the slenderness of the construction, would have surpassed his other, similar stair towers in their elegance. When this design was not constructed, Belgian architecture was robbed of a remarkable building.

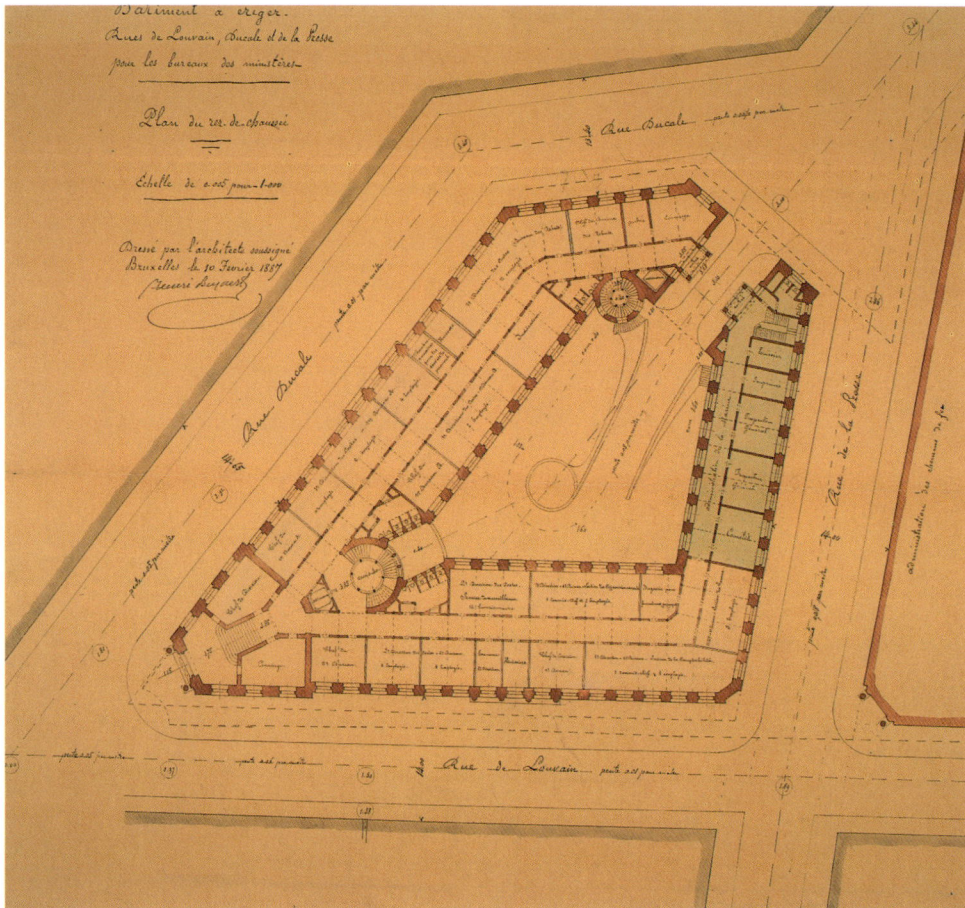

Plan of the building for the Post Office and the Office of Marine Affairs, as designed by Beyaert in 1887, adopted to a great extent by Benoit.

THE HÔTEL DES POSTES ET DE LA MARINE,
BASED ON A CONCEPT BY BENOIT, 1895-1987

Before the year of Beyaert's death was out, the architect Joseph Joachim Benoit, the Chief Architect of the Special Department of Civil Buildings in Brussels, was commissioned to complete his project. Benoit had in fact already headed the construction of Beyaert's Ministry of Railways from the beginning.

After his studies at the Academy of Fine Arts in Brussels, Benoit (1846-1910) entered the Department of Bridges and Roads at the age of seventeen. In 1865 he found himself in the design studio for the building of the new Law Courts in Brussels. He worked there for twelve years under Joseph Poelaert. After the latter's death in 1877 Benoit was made artistic head of the construction of the Law Courts. He completed this difficult assignment in 1883. His gratitude to Poelaert was expressed in his design for the great man's bur-

Benoit's design for the facade of the Hôtel des Postes et de la Marine (1895). The projecting bays, which replace Beyaert's triumphal arch, refer back to Dewez' grand facade.

ial monument in the graveyard in Laken, a reduced version of the entrance to the Law Courts. The direct influence of Poelaert is visible in Benoit's own works, including the grammar school in Verviers and the Academy of Drawing in St. Jans Molenbeek.

When Benoit was assigned to take over Beyaert's project, he declared himself not to be competent to criticize the artistic quality of Beyaert's work. Nevertheless, the ultimate results of his work were only a faint reflection of Beyaert's original design. It was radically simplified and deprived of its most characteristic parts.

Benoit considered it should all be much more rational. The architecture of the building should in the first place correspond to its administrative function. According to some, in his exuberant architecture for the Railways building, Beyaert had failed in this respect. So in his new plans, Benoit linked up again with the architecture of the new ministry buildings, which were emphatically inspired by the eighteenth-century architecture of the district.

The restored vestibule of the present visitors and staff entrance to the Flemish Parliament building at 27 Leuvenseweg, with its marbling and mosaic floor.

◄

The ceiling of the restored vestibule.

►

In the context of this uniform architecture the Palace of the Nation counted as the high point in terms of form, whose example all subsequent building was to follow. So the height of the façades and the ridge line, and even the diameter of the columns in Beyaert's design were meticulously reduced where they exceeded those of the parliament building.

Beyaert's cylindrical stair tower was replaced by straight stair blocks, which were considered more comfortable. The ordonnance of the façades on the Leuvenseweg was given a more 'classical' articulation, with a bossed base, colossal piers in front of the upper floors and a continuous attic storey. According to Benoit, it was in the continued building of what he still considered to be the most successful part of Beyaert's design, the projecting corner bays on the Leuvenseweg, that the Louis XVI style was most closely emulated. The positioning and rhythm of the facade was retained, with its accentuation by balconies every three bays.

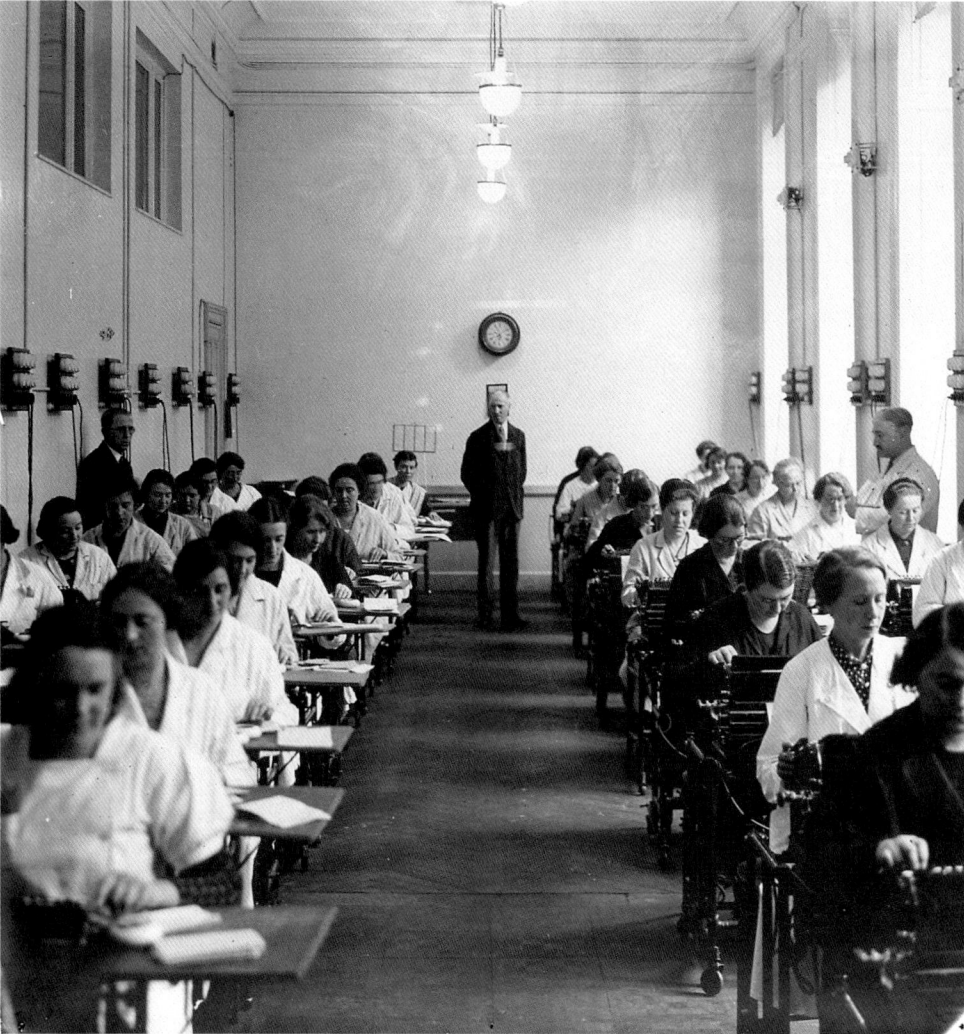

This photo from 1936 shows the working conditions in the 'Salle des machines à additioner' in the old Postcheque building: ladies diligently adding under the supervision of three gentlemen...
◄

The bustle at the counters on the ground floor of the Postcheque building in 1936. This room has now been turned into the Hall of Pillars.
▶

Conversely, Benoit did not adopt the open triumphal arch Beyaert had intended to set on the axis of the Hertogstraat, a three-storey high arcade spanned with 'porte-à-faux', a massive attic storey and a truncated helm roof in the best 'beaux-arts' tradition, and undoubtedly the most striking part of the design. Benoit was uncertain about the effect of this construction which he considered rather excessive. He saw it as totally separate from the rest of the building, both architecturally and in terms of content, as if it were a city gate. Moreover, according to Benoit the triumphal arch took up too much space, and cramped internal movement. At this point Benoit returned almost literally to Dewez' then still existing grand facade, with its round-arched entrance, balcony, colossal Ionic columns, a triangular fronton in the upper building and a balustrade with urns to top it off.

It does however plead for Beyaert that it was precisely the most functional part of his design, the structure and interior divisions, that were adopted in their entirety, never having come under discussion in the Railways building either. In Beyaert's concept, fixed elements such as vestibules, staircases and sanitary facilities were grouped at the ends of the wings. This meant that all the remaining space remained as unrestricted as possible. Movable internal walls enabled the division of this space to be totally flexible, a principle that was to be copied in the building of offices. The architectural structure corresponded to this, being a skeleton of iron girders supported by cast iron columns arranged with a regular bay width of 3.2 metres.

In practice the division of the building for the Post and Marine Affairs broadly speaking amounted to a succession of office spaces on both sides of the central corridor. It was only in the narrower wing on the Drukpersstraat, where the more spacious offices for the more important civil servants were grouped, that the corridor was on the side of the courtyard. On the first floor, accessible by a monumental staircase, the directors of the Post had a richly decorated conference room and a suite of distinguished offices.

Benoit's plans for the building of the Post and the Office of Marine Affairs were approved in 1895. Work started immediately after the demolition work had finished. The contractors, Degendesch-Nachez and Delit-Vermeylen completed the structural work in 1901. The building was only fully completed in 1905.

From 1913 the Hôtel des Postes et de la Marine also housed the newly established Postcheque Board. In 1951 the Postcheque organization moved into a more spacious office building, one of the later works of Victor Bourgeois, designed between 1938 and 1940, between the IJzerenkruisstraat and the Leuvenseweg. The former Hôtel des Postes et de la Marine, owned by the Building Directorate, was, as already mentioned, bought by the Flemish Council for a symbolic frank in 1987. In 1991 this body also acquired the Postcheque building.

The Hall of Pillars derives its name a from a double row of original cast iron pillars. Together with a double row of monumental ceiling lights, they dominate the Hall of Pillars. Powerfully described motifs in the two-colour natural wood parquet give the room an almost Moorish appearance.

▶

3

The bold architecture of the Flemish Parliament building

The story of the design stages, the building and the interior design of the Flemish Parliament building is a fascinating one. It started with the purchase of the Hôtel des Postes et de la Marine in 1987. The choice of partial conservation, sometimes with meticulous restoration, but in the main a resolutely contemporary design, led to a radical renovation which ultimately took much longer than originally planned. As the Flemish Parliament building, the old 'Hôtel' acquired a striking new architectural form, to which the interior, the furnishing and works of art are all attuned in total harmony.

From dream to reality

Just as ten years were needed for the design and building stages of the Hôtel des Postes et de la Marine (1895-1905), almost a decade passed between the acquisition of the building by the Flemish Council in 1987 and the end of the renovation in spring 1996. During the final stages, there was great pressure

Plan of the ground floor of the Flemish Parliament building, with entrance and circulation zones in grey, communal areas in ochre (clockwise: Anna Bijns Room, Coffee Room and Hall of Pillars), and the hall for plenary meetings in green. The mezzanine floor houses the press zone.

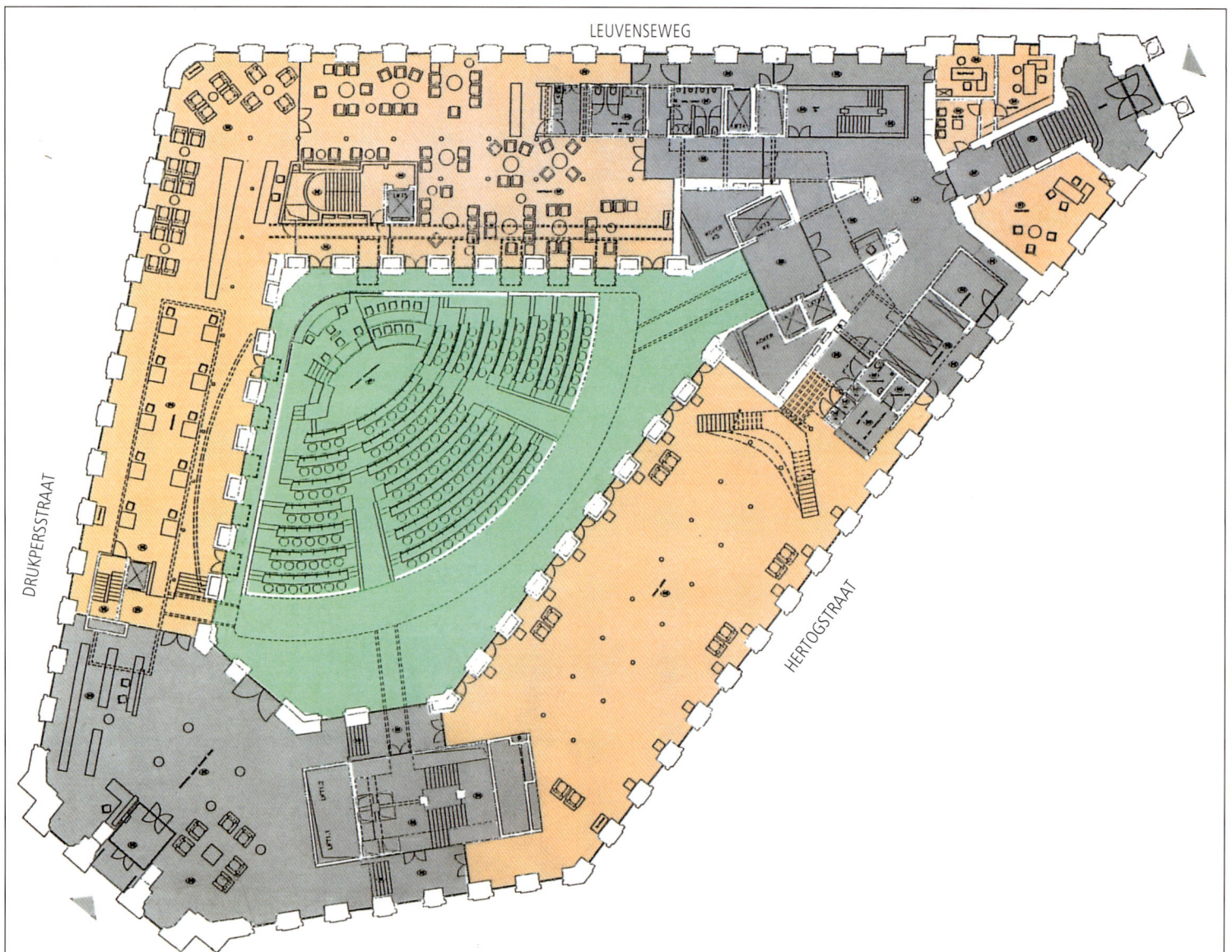

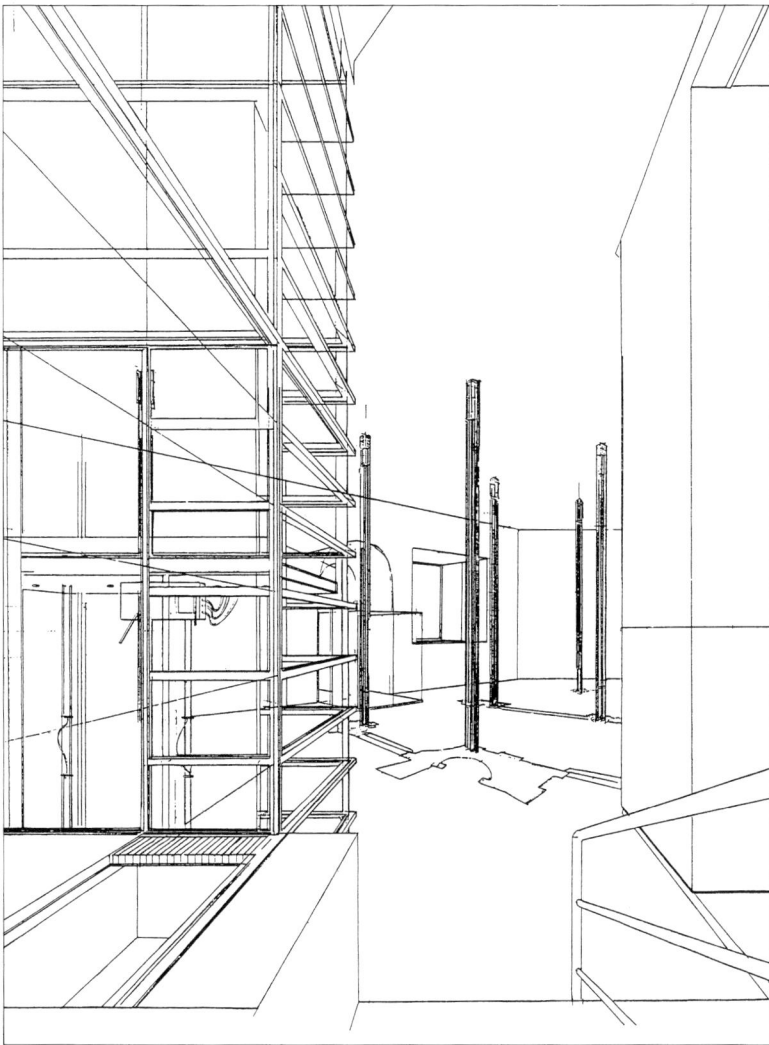

Perspective drawing of the peristyle on the Hertogstraat side, with the outlines of the walls of the former carriage entrance worked into the floor.

from the Flemish MPs, who had been directly elected for the first time in May 1995. They wanted to bring this long-awaited house of their own into use, to be able to work under optimum conditions at last. The Flemish Parliament building was officially opened on Saturday 16th and Sunday 17th March 1996. This was preceded by a media campaign never before associated with a parliament. No less than six thousand visitors were counted that weekend: interested Flemish people, the media and official guests. The misery of the building process was in the past.

In the preceding years the frequently heard and appropriate adage was that 'One does not build a parliament everyday'. There are no ready-made models for building a parliament. It was no simple matter for the Flemish Council to lay down a definitive building programme. The successive state reforms regularly expanded its task. So the infrastructural needs had to be constantly reformulated. For a long time even the number of MPs remained uncertain, and this is the very first fundamental piece of information needed. To paraphrase William Elsschot's verse, *'Between dream and reality stood the maker of the constitution and practical difficulties'*.

The basis for an initial study of the requirements in the mid-eighties was a Flemish Parliament with extended areas of competence linked to the population, and limited regional authority. At that time it was still assumed that the entire parliamentary infrastructure, its chambers and specific needs such as the library, as well as all the offices of the parliament, could be concentrated in the new building.

The 1988 and 1993 state reforms transformed the Flemish assembly into a genuinely full parliament. This signified a substantial increase in the number of staff, both in its own departments and those of the parliamentary parties. The original plans for the arrangement of the parliament building did not provide for this. In the end the Bureau decided to buy a second building for the departments. So once again space was released in the parliament building itself.

On each occasion the building programme and the organization of the space had to be adapted to these changes. This was ultimately to the advantage of the presentation and communal areas and the reception rooms. At the same time this avoided the problem that an overloaded building programme might be to the detriment of the architecture.

In order to solve the lack of space, in 1991 the Flemish Council bought the complex of buildings that formed the headquarters of the Postcheque Department, between the IJzerenkruisstraat and the Leuvenseweg, directly opposite the Flemish Parliament building. Most of the departments and the offices of the Flemish MPs and their staff will be housed in this spacious complex. Thorough renovation and conversion work is also planned for that building. They will be completed in about 2000.

An initial sketch of the present visitors entrance at 27 Leuvenseweg, containing the pillars of the former vestibule: a confrontation of old and new.

The architectural concept

Apart from the adaptations necessary as a result of the changes to the institution, the architectural concept also underwent a thorough metamorphosis in its preparatory stages, in terms of both form and content.

The design of the architecture and the interior was entrusted to the architects Willy Verstraete, from the Arrow engineering office in Ghent, and Jozef Fuyen from the architectural firm of the same name, in Antwerp. The idea was originally of a concept in which only the outer walls of the building would be preserved, because no room for plenary meetings could be built within the existing space. This would have been a convenient solution, a work of 'façadism', which had in recent years given architecture a worthless character, particularly in Brussels. A determined search was made for a meaningful way of handling the existing architecture. In the end the designers opted for the optimum retention or reuse of all the valuable elements.

The Flemish Parliament building was not and is still not a classified monument in the legal sense. But its historical nature and its location in the Warande District make it natural that any conversion had to have the approval of the Brussels Royal Commission for Monuments and Landscapes. The dialogue with the commission resulted in an inventory of rooms whose preservation was a priority, including the former Post Office council chamber, a number of directors' offices, and the architecturally interesting staircase

Detail of a wall covered in warm red leather in the Bureau Room. It could well be a painting by Mondriaan.

▼

The Coffee Room for the Flemish MPs. The press, other staff and civil servants have no access here.

near the Leuvenseweg entrance. It was also decided to retain the outer façades and doors, the inner façades and the original floor levels. It was possible to build an attic floor with a mansard roof under the height of the existing ridge, as long as it was not too visible above the upper façades. This meant the original plan for a new, fourth floor had to be dropped.

The architects opted on the one hand for meaningful conservation, while on the other resolutely deciding to add new structures. The designs for these were markedly contemporary, but without crudeness. The new contribution became highly recognizable, partly as a result of a rational choice of materials.

The architects decided on the extensive use of glass. Intentionally or not, this accentuates transparency and is symbolic of the political culture the

Flemish Parliament wishes to propagate. The old building, whose massive, stately appearance is intended to command respect, has been given an added contemporary credibility. A successful architectural dialogue between old and new.

The use of glass and metal, in many cases stainless steel, has kept all the new interventions as separate as possible from the existing structure. The existing skeleton of steel girders and cast-iron pillars that lay hidden behind the building's formal classical appearance was upgraded where possible. The architects' original intention had been to expose the skeleton completely, to allow it to play its part as a visible, structuring element in the architecture of the interior. But the necessity of hanging false ceilings, thereby concealing the girder structure, meant this captivating and rational option was no longer possible. The remaining pillars today give a new rhythm, mainly to the corridors, though they do seem rather out of context.

Nevertheless, the confrontation between existing and contemporary elements has led to a new arrangement that opens up interesting and often surprising views through the building.

Detail of Liliane Vertessen's controversial work of art entitled 'Never the same, always different' in the Hans Memling Room. If you read by colour, it says 'Never different, always the same'...

Apart from the hall for plenary meetings, whose scale and desired allure prevented it from being fitted into the structure of the building, all necessary functions were housed in the existing rooms. The complex programme comprises among other things a study and reading room and a coffee room for the MPS, reception rooms, the offices of the Speaker and Secretary General, offices for the members of the Bureau and their staff, a press room and workrooms for journalists, offices for the secretarial staff of the various parliamentary parties and a great many committee rooms.

Much attention was paid to the arrangement of the interior, which lends support to both the function and the design of the building. The choice of materials is consistently maintained. Striking examples of this are the parquet floors which, due to the use of two types of wood (pine and a tropical hardwood), sometimes display splendid forms, and the specially designed monumental hanging lights that adorn various parts of both the restored and the contemporary areas. The same applies to the furni-

The Shell, the impressive multifunctional space under the Domed Hall, for receptions and colloquiums.

◀

ture, which Willy Verstraete also played a part in designing: it has a modern form and is always adapted to the specific character and function of the room. The material chosen, pear wood, gives it a feeling of uniformity. This is again reinforced by the use of the same *'parliamentary chair'* in all the meeting rooms, ergonomically designed and upholstered in practical beige leather, with aluminium arm-rests, and with a foot that is softened by strips of inlaid pear wood.

Art in the Flemish Parliament

Works of art play a very special part in the Flemish Parliament building. The Bureau was advised in its choice of artists by the *'Committee for the Integration of Works of Art'*, specially set up for the purpose and composed of prominent art experts.

A number of contemporary Flemish artists were requested to create a work of art for specific locations or for various rooms. This involved frequent consultation between the artists and the architects.

Today the visitor can see works by Fred Bervoets, Bert De Beul, Ronny Delrue, Denmark, Hugo Duchateau, Fred Eerdekens, Jan Fabre, Vic Gentils, Marie-Jo Lafontaine, Roger Raveel, Pjeero Roobjee, Paul Sochaki, Gilbert Swimberghe, Narcisse Tordoir, Camiel Van Breedam, Paul Van Hoeydonck, Liliane Vertessen and Mark Verstockt.

The presence of works of art in cleverly selected positions increases the number of surprising, sometimes playful effects so characteristic of the building. They accentuate even more the contemporary character of the interior. Some of the works of art have an immediate appeal, while others fascinate or intrigue, need time to be grasped, or incite controversy. More than one of the artists used the opportunity presented to make an ironic or critical comment on the political world. As is always the case in art, only time will tell which works of art will be seen to be of permanent significance.

The Flemish Parliament will also continue to purchase rigorously selected works in the future, as well as offering commissions to Flemish artists, though at a more modest tempo. The integration of these works into the spatial environment will always be of prime importance.

A number of works of art by Flemish artists which the parliament purchased between 1976 and 1980 to adorn the then corridors and offices have now also been used in the Flemish Parliament building. These include works by Jan Burssens, Gerard Gaudaen, Pol Mara, Joris Minne, Rik Poot, Luc Peire, Roger Somville, Hilde Van Sumere, Jan Yoors and Roger Wittewrongel, as well as a 'Zelfgave' by Felix de Boeck, a gift from the artist to the Flemish Parliament.

Jan Fabre created this characteristic sculptural work for the Hall of Pillars: human figures covered in glittering Oriental scarabs, freeze-dried insects from Eastern countries. The work is un-titled. According to the artist they represent fallen angels. As in ancient Egypt, the insects stand for hope and life.

▶

The Constant Permeke Room, one of the smaller committee rooms, which is twinned with the Valerius De Saedeleer Room.

▼

Art in the Flemish Parliament

Levels -1 & -2

The Shell
MARK VERSTOCKT,
Caduceus (1995)
aluminium and stainless steel

Frans Masereel Room
DENMARK,
Die Welt im Griff (1986)
newsprint, wood

Ground Floor

Hall of Pillars
JAN FABRE,
Untitled
beetles and wire

Anna Bijns Room
VIC GENTILS,
Omaggio a Boccioni
and *Metamorphosis II* (1986)
wood on pedestal, polychrome

Mezzanine Floor

Corridor
FRED BERVOETS,
De vier vrouwen (The Four Women)
(1991)
raised etching, paper, canvas

First Floor

Bureau Room
HUGO DUCHATEAU,
Vlaanderen in de wereld (Flanders in
the World) (1995)
brass

Rik Wouters Room
PAUL VAN HOEYDONCK,
Planeet (Planet) (1993-1995)
bronze

In front of the Speaker's office
ROGER RAVEEL,
Bezinning over de illusie van de macht
(Reflection on the Illusion of Power)
(1995)
oil paint on canvas, mirrors and
mixed media

Second Floor

Jeroen Bosch Room
BERT DE BEUL,
Untitled (1995)
oil paint on canvas

James Ensor Room
RONNY DELRUE,
reflecties (Reflections) (1996)
acrylic paint on canvas / plaster figures

Constant Permeke Room
PAUL SOCHACKI,
Untitled (1995)
enamel on steel sheet

Valerius De Saedeleer Room
GILBERT SWIMBERGHE,
4 composities (4 Compositions)
(1994-1995)
oil paint on canvas

*Hans Memling Room and
Quinten Metsijs Room*
LILIANE VERTESSEN,
Yoshua Tree and *Nooit hetzelfde,
altijd anders* (Never the same,
always different) (1995)
mixed media

Adjacent to the Peter Paul Rubens Room
MARIE-JO LAFONTAINE,
*The red monochrome, The blue mono-
chrome, The green monochrome,* and
The pink monochrome (1995)
oil paint on wood

Corridor
PJEEROO ROOBJEE,
*Man met vele eigenschappen of de
dichter in Nieuw Westerbork* (Man of
Many Qualities, or the Poet in Nieuw
Westerbork) (1995)
oil paint on canvas

Third Floor

Pieter Bruegel Room
NARCISSE TORDOIR,
Untitled (1995)
mixed media

Jan Van Eyck Room
FRED EERDEKENS,
Er zijn zaken en er zijn bijzaken (There
are Issues and there are Side-Issues)
(1995)
brass wire, light/no light

Corridor
CAMIEL VAN BREEDAM,
Horen, zien, zwijgen
(Hear, see, say nothing) (1995)
assemblage, mixed media

The Anna Bijns Room, named after the sixteenth-
century Antwerp poetess, is the Flemish MPs'
reading room and study. Here they can read the
newspapers and periodicals and consult the
reports of the Belga Agency online. The mezzanine floor houses the press workrooms.

▶

A guided tour along pillars and through halls...

The floor plan of the Flemish Parliament building reveals a compact complex of buildings in the form of an irregular hexagon, bounded by the Hertogstraat, the Leuvenseweg and the Drukpersstraat. At its centre there was a courtyard, and this is now the location of the *Domed Hall*, the room for plenary meetings. This room is the building's epicentre.

Go through the main entrance to the peristyle (literally 'a room with columns') and one is faced with a monumental entrance hall with six massive pillars and the outlines of the walls of the former carriage entrance worked into the bluestone floor. The reception desk and the cloakroom for the Flemish MPs and visitors are discretely arranged. *The peristyle* offers fine perspective views of the adjacent rooms, which remain separated from each other by auditive and visual filters. Despite its obvious monumentality the visitor experiences a feeling of security. Striking features are the completely free-

▲

Panoramic view of the peristyle, literally the 'hall of pillars', on the Hertogstraat side.

View up the panoramic lift shaft in the peristyle, which cuts through five floors in stainless steel and glass.

▶

standing lift shaft and staircase in stainless steel and glass. The shaft cuts vertically through the building; taking the lift offers one a fascinating visual spectacle.

Past the lift shaft is the former counter area of the Postcheque offices, which is now the *Hall of Pillars*. The room owes its name to a double row of original cast-iron pillars. Together with a double row of monumental ceiling lights they dominate the Hall of Pillars. Powerfully described motifs in the two-tone natural wood parquet floor give the room an almost Moorish look. The sparse furnishings are deliberately kept restrained. In the centre there hangs a work of art by Jan Fabre, typical of his recent sculptural work: three female figures made out of wire and Oriental scarabs in various shades, a mass of glittering insects. The insects are symbolic of hope and life. This work of art reflects only one aspect of the work of this artistic jack of all trades who also creates plays, operas and ballets, whose work is internationally esteemed and can be found in numerous museums both at home and abroad. The Hall of Pillars is used as a reception room for various purposes.

Beyond the Hall of Pillars lies the present *public and staff entrance* in the Leuvenseweg. The original vestibule and marble grand staircase, which bridges the difference of height with the main entrance in the Hertogstraat, were rigorously conserved. The painted marble – the well-known 'faux-marbre' technique, the woodwork, the mosaic floor and the plaster ceiling were restored to their former glory. It is ironic that in the nineteenth century, marbling often replaced the rare and expensive marble, whereas today this *painted marble* has become almost prohibitively expensive due to the craftsmen's higher wages. And those skilled workers who are capable of using this technique are scarcer than the rarest of marbles. The staircase further up, connecting to the upper floors, was replaced by a staircase in stainless steel and glass, to echo the lift shaft and staircase next to the peristyle, as described above.

Detail of the staircase, an impression of blue-stone, stainless steel and glass.

◀

The original cast-iron columns give an unusual rhythm to the corridors, accentuated even more by the discrete lighting by spots at the foot of each column.

▶

Detail of the vestibule on the Leuvenseweg side.

▼

General view of Roger Raveel's 'Reflection on the Illusion of Power'.

The first floor is occupied mainly by the offices of the Speaker, the Secretary General and the members of the Bureau and their staff. This is the floor that most exudes the atmosphere of the former Post Office ministry.

The former council chamber, now the *Speaker's office*, also used to be the most important room in the building. It has been restored to its former state. The original paintwork, a combination of marbling and stencilled ornamentation in pastel shades, had to be completely reconstructed, as it had disintegrated, due in part to inadequate measures to protect it during the long building process. The Belgian lion, which formerly adorned the coat of arms, was replaced by the Flemish lion, the arms of the Flemish Community. The fine decoration of this former Post Office council chamber, with its rows of pilasters and columns, looks out onto the Hertogstraat.

Roger Raveel was commissioned to design a work of art for the broad space in front of the Speaker's office. It was to become a monumental piece, using oil paint on canvas, mirrors and mixed media, and is called *Bezinning over de illusie van de macht* (Reflection on the Illusion of Power). The artist made use of the freedom he was offered to set his reflections here, in the close prox-

The Rik Wouters Room with Paul Van Hoeydonck's 'Planet'.

The Peter Paul Rubens Room.

imity of power, symbolized by the Speaker's office. This work of art demands attention, raises questions and makes a lasting impression.

Further along the corridor is the *Bureau Room*, undoubtedly one of the finest rooms in the Flemish Parliament building. This is where the Bureau and the Extended Bureau meet. The work of art above the monumental round table is Hugo Duchateau's *Vlaanderen in de wereld*. The world is represented by a large circular structure in brass. In this work, Flanders is the smallest ring-shaped piece that has its place in the world. The horns symbolize not only dialogue with each other, but also listening to each other. This work of art is a plea for communication between little Flanders and the big world. The images of the animals on the ring refer to the various continents, as well as to the animal species which, just like humans, have to live in harmony with each other if they wish to survive.

The former directors' offices on the first floor, whose decoration was limited to head-high panelling and inlaid parquet, have been given a thorough facelift. They are now the offices of the Deputy Speakers and Secretaries of the Flemish Parliament. The pillars give the corridors a very unusual, exceptional rhythm, which is further accentuated by discrete lighting by spots at the foot of each pillar.

The section of corridor between the Bureau Room and the *Rik Wouters Room*, clad in bright red leather, provides this floor with an attractive and recognizable feature.

Ten *committee rooms* were created on the second and third floors. All of them bear the names of celebrated Flemish

The Bureau Room, one of the most harmonious rooms. Hugo Duchateau's 'Flanders in the World' is fully integrated into the room.

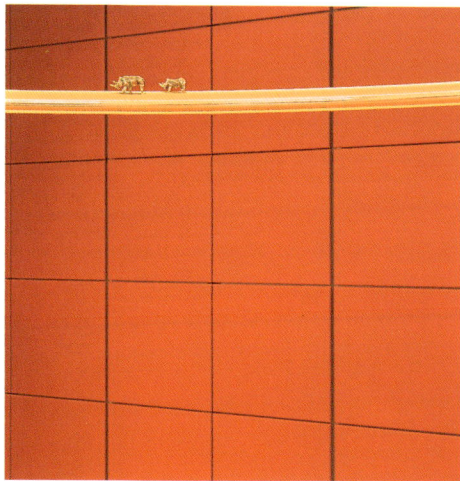

painters, from Jan Van Eyck to Constant Permeke. The choice of the names of old masters is in itself a deliberate contrast to the works of contemporary Flemish art that adorn most of the rooms. The rooms vary in size and are suitable for meetings for 20 to 60 people. The four largest committee rooms are at the corners of the building, in the form of gently raked theatres. The *Jan Van Eyck Room* is undoubtedly the most striking, dominated by the original steel roof beams with a notable array of suspended lamps. A decidedly intriguing feature is Fred Eerdekens' work of art, *Er zijn zaken en er zijn bijzaken* (There are Issues and there are Side-Issues). The artist mounted seemingly whimsical forms in brass wire a few centimetres from the two side walls. The way the lights are focused on the wire enable the visitor to read fragments of

The Jan Van Eyck Room, the most striking committee room.

Intriguing: Fred Eerdekens' 'There are Issues and there are Side-Issues', created using brass wire and... light.

▶

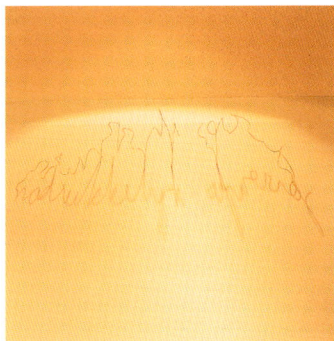

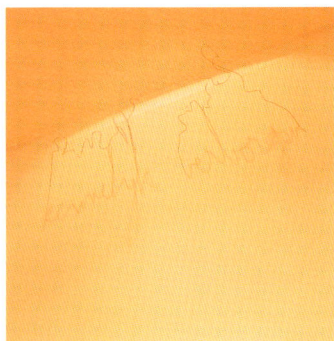

sentences, such as 'remarkably subtle', 'possibly superfluous', 'pointedly absent', 'obviously concealed' and 'apparently by chance'. The technique is certainly original anyway, and the artist offers his thoughts, with an acute sense of perspective, on the walls of a room where the real parliamentary work is done. This is a good example of the social-critical role of contemporary art. The Jan Van Eyck Room is furthermore the most completely equipped committee room. Among all the technical, visual and auditive auxiliary equipment, the most striking are the interpreters' boxes along the back wall. The *Pieter Brueghel Room* also deserves a special mention for Narcisse Toudoir's work *Untitled*: thirty-two strictly ordered, multicoloured little panels each with a different motifs, against a black and white background, give the room a very special atmosphere.

Six smaller committee rooms, linked two by two, form mirror images of each other. By linking the entrances of these twin rooms to each other, recognizable points are created that enable the users to find their way by instinct. These entrances are all made in a combination of glass and pear wood, with a blue marble floor element in the form of a circle or a trapezium in front of the doors. The gleaming marble areas shine out in the midst of the parquet floor of the corridors. The glass allows one a discrete look into the rooms. All these small, tastefully selected accents prevent the corridors becoming monotonous. The names of these twin-rooms also form couples, being the names of Flemish painters of the same era or with the same themes. So we see *Constant Permeke* with *Valerius De Saedeleer*, *Jeroen Bosch* with *James Ensor*, and *Hans Memling* with *Quinten Metsijs*.

This last set of two rooms offers the greatest contrast. Anyone thinking of the serene work of the old masters is confronted with two works by Liliane Vertessen, called *Yoshua Tree* and *Nooit anders, altijd hetzelfde* (Never the same, always different), for which the artist used photography, mirrors and neon lights. The *Quinten Metsijs Room* is dominated by a bright green text written in neon, *Love yourself so you can love somebody else*, and this is set against a mirrored wall the breadth of the room. In the *Hans Memling Room*, again against a mirrored wall, one can read *Nooit hetzelfde, altijd anders* in red and white neon. But if one follows the words by colour it reads *Nooit anders, altijd hetzelfde*. The works by this internationally known artist undoubtedly elicit the most comment, even controversy. The warm furnishings of the twin-rooms are also linked: either circular, or oval or bisected oval tables. The play of lines in the fixed furnishings makes each of the twin-rooms easily identifiable.

The Quinten Metsijs Room and the Hans Memling Room are twinned. Liliane Vertessen created a controversial work of art for both these rooms.

◄

The entrances to the Hans Memling and Quinten Metsijs Rooms. The gleaming marble flooring element shines out of the parquet floor of the corridors.

►

The third floor is intended for the offices of the parliamentary parties. In addition to a limited amount of office space, the new metal roof structure houses the technical installations.

... and look up at the sky

The crowning architectural glory, which gives the Flemish Parliament building an undeniable grandeur, is the plenary assembly hall or *Domed Hall*, the epicentre of the whole project. The 124 Flemish MPs, the nine Flemish ministers, the officials from the ministerial offices, the press and the public all have their clearly marked areas, parts of an all-embracing, unifying space oriented towards mutual communication. The original façades of this former polygonal courtyard now form part of the outer walls of the hall. The excavation of the courtyard two floors below ground level created a broad space roofed over at first floor height using a glass structure composed of triangles. This dome, with the same shape as the courtyard, is at the present time unique. It spans a space 39 by 25 metres, or an area of 645 m², and weighs at least 72 tons, though there is no visible structure supporting it. The 807 glass elements function like a vault, holding each other up in space. The great lateral pressure exercised by the dome meant that the whole structure had to be supported by columns in the walls round the courtyard. In order to achieve this, the walls all round the space were demolished and rebuilt.

The architects had originally thought of a flat glass ceiling set above the cornice of the courtyard's façades, which would have emphasized even more the intrinsic qualities of the yard. They later opted for a dome. There was for some time discussion on where it should be located – at cornice height, or at the present height above the ground floor. The latter option was selected for reasons of energy conservation. The structure of the dome itself evolved, as a

result of technical difficulties, from a lighter, square grid structure to the present, triangular pattern.

The form of this dome, curving in all directions, produces a double, almost contradictory effect. On the one hand there is tremendous feeling of openness – one literally sees the sky and the façades of the courtyard – and on the other a feeling of security and compactness. Daylight illuminates both the speakers and the listeners, prolonged debates become more bearable, there is contact with the outside world, and one has visual contact with events in the plenary assembly hall from the surrounding rooms.

The reflection of light on the glass elements means one cannot look into the Domed Hall from above during the day. But in the evening the brightly lit assembly hall provides a magical spectacle. Those in the Domed Hall experience the effect in reverse: during the day they see the sky, and at night the dome becomes a black cocoon with dozens of halogen spots on the inside. At twilight the two effects gradually dissolve into each other, an image that has inspired many a photographer. Technically speaking, the relatively low level of the dome leads to low energy consumption, the acoustic glass prevents long reverberations or 'whisper effect', and the type of glass selected reflects most of the warmth of the sun. A powerful air conditioning installation does the rest.

A second, equally powerful architectural image is provided by the shell form which, like the palm of a giant hand, contains the broad quarter circle in a gently curving slope. The concrete shell is supported by a central pillar under the rostrum and seven bulky angled columns. They determine the appearance of the multifunctional room below, which is appropriately called *The Shell*. The negative form of the concrete shell forms its roof, and the elongated foundations of the inner façades of the courtyard form the walls. The rough yellow-ochre coloured acoustic finish of The Shell itself, and the openings for spots cut into its girth, give it a strangely attractive and even intimate character, despite its enormous space. Seen from the underground multifunctional space, the shell, which stands completely free from the surrounding façades, appears to be floating. The architects had in fact originally argued for the best possible use of this striking visual effect, and not to disrupt it by building a division between the levels above and under the ground.

However, the requirement to be able use The Shell and the Domed Hall at the same time meant that an auditive screen was in any case essential. For this reason a glass floor was laid round the shell at ground floor level, supported by a steel structure, which provides the MPs access to their seats

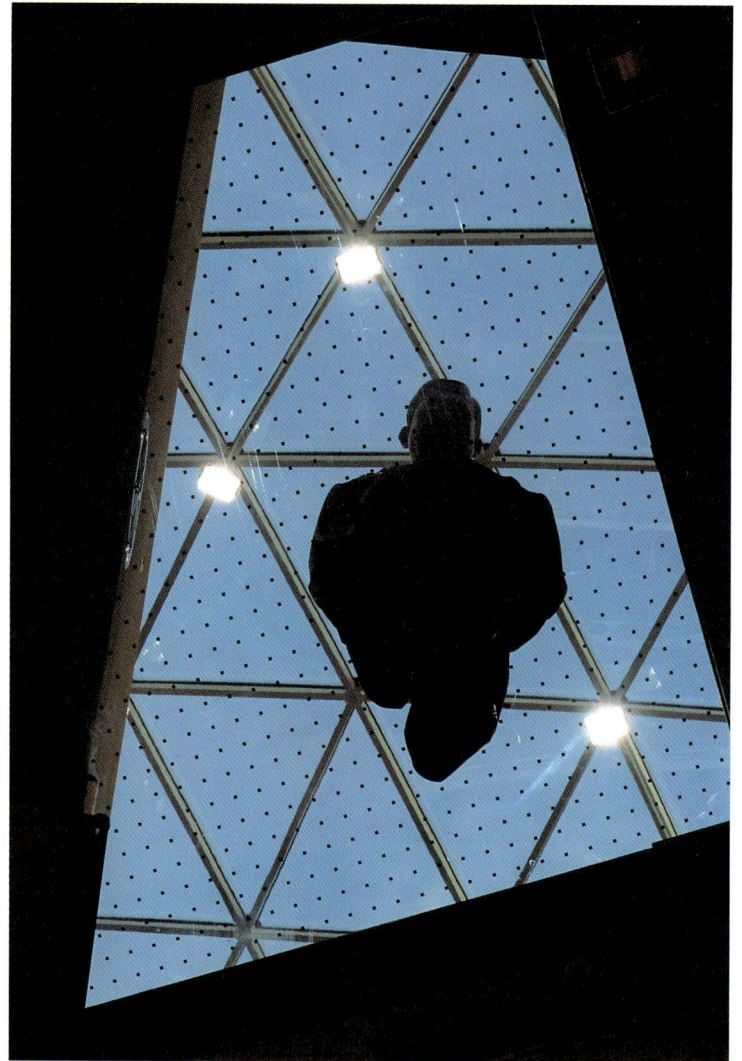

instead of the catwalks which had originally been planned. The conical pro-
file of the steel structure originally designed by the architects, which presented a minimal visual obstacle, had to be strengthened during construction
for technical reasons, which somewhat lessened the effect of the 'glass' floor.
Even so, this transparent level guarantees the space beneath sufficient daylight and creates fascinating views through to the Domed hall and the façades
of the courtyard.

The white marble floor inlaid with small stainless steel circles is traversed
by two black marble stripes, whose intersection indicates the position of the
Flemish Parliament on the globe: 50 degrees, 50 minutes, 51 seconds North
latitude and 4 degrees, 22 minutes, 3 seconds East longitude. This original ori-
entation point involuntarily strengthens the impression of anchoring which
was already powerfully created by the sturdy concrete columns as if they had
been driven into the Brussels ground. It involuntarily but emphatically accentuates the bond between Flanders and the Brussels Flemings in the Flemish
capital, Brussels.

The forceful lines of The Shell.
▶

The Shell is a reception room for, among other things, the annual 11th of July celebrations, although exhibitions and colloquiums can also be mounted there. Mark Verstockt's monumental work of art, called *Caduceus*, made of aluminium and steel, provides a major point of interest above the rostrum.

A worn-out office building, doomed to be demolished, with its rather dull, deliberately faceless architecture, which was symbolic of an outdated patriarchal past, has been given a new zest by means of a radical renovation. The

The white marble floor of The Shell, with its small inlaid stainless steel circles, is traversed by two black marble stripes. Their intersection indicates the geographical position of the Flemish Parliament: 50 degrees, 50 minutes, 51 seconds North latitude and 4 degrees, 22 minutes 3 seconds East longitude.

intrinsic qualities of the old building provided the basis, and the bold contemporary interventions gave it the superstructure of a strong architectural concept. The forceful shape of the triple epicentre, the dome, the shell and the space below, the lightness of the ubiquitous glass, the earnestness of the restoration, the modern design of the architecture and the furnishings, and the highly individual works of art make the Flemish Parliament building a lasting monument, for both the Flemish MPs and for Flanders.

The concrete shell of the hall for plenary meetings and part of the dome, reflected in the glass floor; and a view through to the multifunctional space below.

4

The Flemish Parliament: the political heart of Flanders

The Flemish Parliament is the political heart of Flanders. Although more attention is often paid to the ministers who govern Flanders on a daily basis, and even though their direct power is greater, the Flemish Parliament ultimately has the last word in Flanders. In this chapter we introduce the reader into the world of Flemish politics, as it is carried on day after day in the attractive open surroundings of the Flemish Parliament building.

124 Flemish Members of Parliament

The Flemish Parliament was directly elected for the first time on 21st May 1995. As explained in chapter 1, the Flemish parliamentary assembly had previously been made up of directly elected Dutch-speaking members of the federal Belgian parliament. The next direct elections for the Flemish Parliament will coincide with the elections for the European and federal parliaments, in June 1999. After that there will only be elections for the Flemish Parliament every five years.

The Flemish Parliament cannot be dissolved before the end of its term. For this reason the Flemish Parliament is known as a fixed term parliament.

The Flemish Parliament has 124 Flemish MPs. 118 of them are directly elected by the inhabitants of the Flemish Region. For the organization of the elections the five provinces of the Flemish Region are divided into eleven constituencies, each of which may return a number of MPs dependent on the population densi-

The Domed Hall, with the arms of the Flemish Community woven into the carpet in front of the Speaker's chair.

▶

The Domed Hall

The plenary assemblies of the Flemish Parliament take place in the Domed Hall. The plenary assembly is the highest organ of the Flemish Parliament. This is where the 124 Flemish MPs come together, and here the political decisions are made whose concrete consequences affect the Flemish people. For instance, the plenary assembly appoints, and if necessary dismisses, the Flemish Government, and votes on the bills submitted by the Flemish Government, as well as the decrees proposed by its own members.

The plenary assembly is chaired by the Speaker of the Flemish Parliament, who sits at the front. Next to him sit the parliamentary secretaries, who are responsible, among other things, for recording the voting results. Members who wish to speak go to the rostrum.

Each parliamentary party has places reserved in the Domed Hall. Every MP has his or her permanent seat.

The Lion of Flanders, the symbol of the Flemish Community, is woven into the carpet at the front.

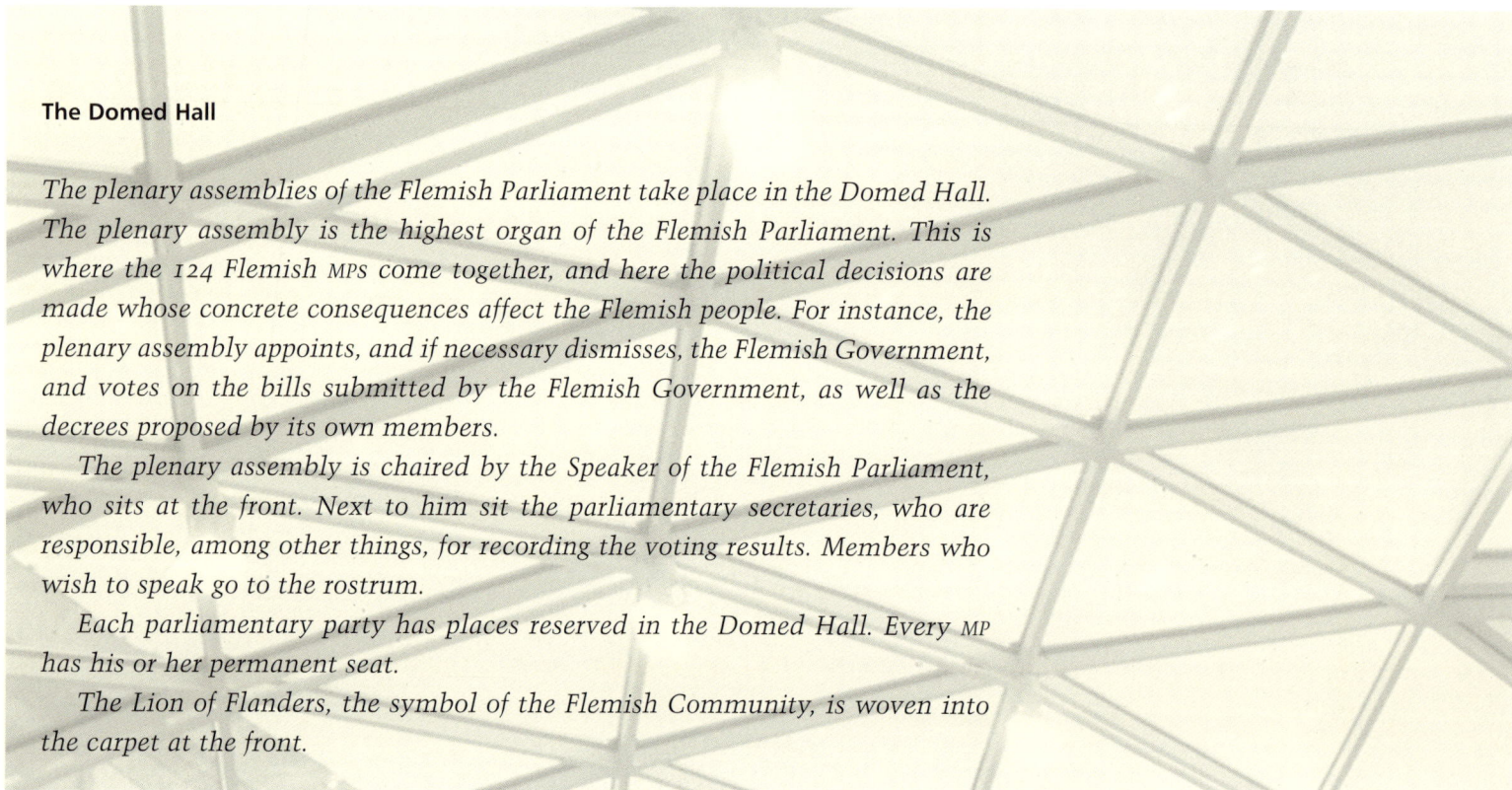

ty. In addition to these MPs, the Flemish Parliament also provides seats for the six first elected Dutch-speaking members of the Brussels parliament. This means the Brussels Flemings are also represented in the Flemish Parliament.

The conditions for candidature to the Flemish Parliament are the same as for the federal parliament, provided that one lives in the Flemish Region. An inhabitant of Liège, for example, cannot be a candidate for the Flemish Parliament. As has been explained, a special arrangement has been worked out for the Brussels Flemings.

When the Flemish Parliament assembles for the first time after an election, there is first an enquiry into whether the members have been elected in accordance with the legal regulations. This is called the *Examination of the Credentials*. After this examination the legally elected MPs take the oath.

The Flemish Parliament returns ten members to the Senate (the upper house). They are called *Community Senators*, and together with their counterparts from the other regional parliaments their task is to guarantee the bond between the federal state and its member states.

The 124 Flemish MPs are in principle members of political parties. At the moment there are seven political parties represented in the Flemish Parliament: the Christelijke Volkspartij (CVP - Christian Democrats), the Vlaamse Liberalen en Democraten (VLD - Liberals), the Socialistische Partij (SP - Socialists), the Vlaams Blok (VB - extreme right), the Volksunie (VU - Flemish Nationalists), Agalev ('Anders gaan leven' - Green) and the Union des Francophones (UF - French speakers). Members who do not belong to a political party sit as independents.

The play of shapes in the warm wooden furniture of the James Ensor Room.

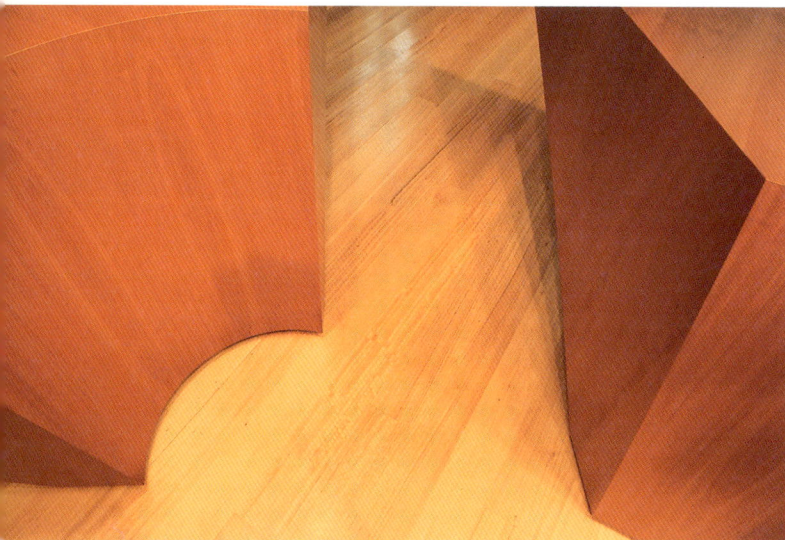

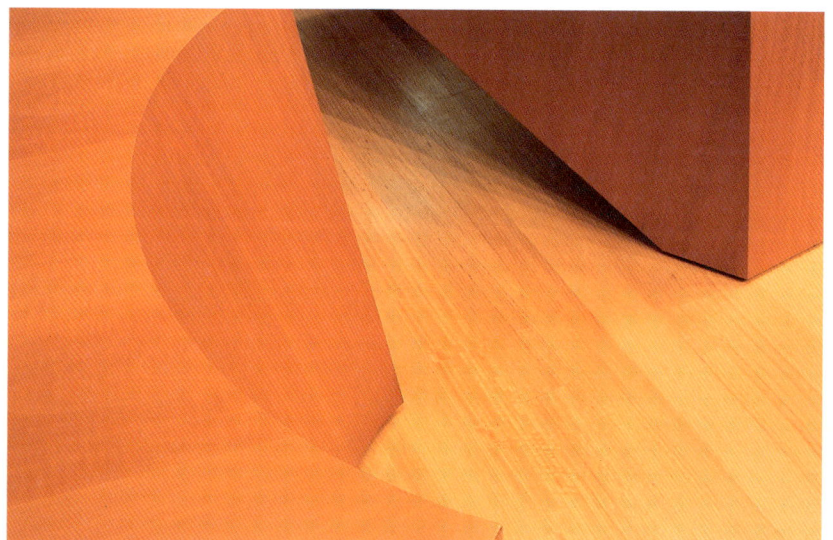

Members of the same party form a *parliamentary party*. Each parliamentary party elects a chairman who acts as the party's spokesman. These parties hold weekly meetings at which they assess the political situation and determine political strategy. The speakers for the coming debates are also designated here, and a voting plan is settled. If a parliamentary party has seven or more members it is granted the resources to establish a secretariat with its own staff.

The tasks of the Flemish MPs

The Flemish MPs have four major tasks. First of all they appoint the Flemish Government, which is responsible for the day to day administration of Flanders. Then, together with the Flemish Government, they determine the development of Flemish society. This is done by passing Flemish laws – *decrees* – which all Flemings must observe. The Flemish Parliament makes available the necessary financial resources for the implementation of the decrees. This is done by the approval of the annual budget, a third major parliamentary task. And finally the Flemish MPs monitor the Flemish Government, which has to implement and enforce the decrees.

Ministers' benches

Ministers are not members of the parliament. Yet the presence of the members of the Flemish Government in the Flemish Parliament is laid down in the constitution: the ministers can explain and defend their policies there, and the MPs can at any time call upon them to justify the policy they are pursuing.

In the committee rooms, a minister will usually sit next to the chairman of the committee. In the Domed Hall there are special 'ministers benches' next to the Speaker's chair, right at the front of the hall. This allows ministers to enter easily into dialogue with the MPs.

It is only MPs who have the right to vote and who take part in voting, not the ministers.

THE FLEMISH PARLIAMENT APPOINTS THE FLEMISH GOVERNMENT

After the elections, and after the Flemish Parliament has been put together, it appoints a maximum of eleven ministers nominated by a majority of Flemish MPs. Together they form the Flemish Government. But the present government only has nine ministers. These ministers are elected by, but not necessarily from, the Flemish MPs. There must be at least one minister who lives in the Brussels region, which requirement once again consolidates the bond between Flanders and the Brussels Flemings.

Immediately after their appointment the ministers of the Flemish Government take the oath before the Speaker of the Flemish Parliament. It is only the Speaker of the Flemish Government, the minister-president, that takes the oath before the King.

The members of the Flemish Government are not members of the Flemish Parliament. A Flemish MP who accepts a ministerial portfolio resigns as a member of the Flemish Parliament and is replaced by his successor for the duration of his term of office.

After the oath has been taken, the Flemish Government makes a *government statement* in the Flemish Parliament in which they explain the main lines of their policy for their term of office. When the government obtains the support of a majority of Flemish MPs, it can start carrying out its programme.

The Domed Hall, with the rostrum on the left, the Speaker's chair in the middle and the ministers benches at the right front.

Together with the Flemish Parliament, the Flemish Government forms the driving force behind the social policy pursued in Flanders. Together with the parliament it prepares the Flemish decrees and, once they are passed, implements them. To implement and monitor the observance of these decrees, the government can issue ministerial orders and has at its disposal the officials of the Ministry of the Flemish Community and the Flemish public bodies.

The voting board

When the Flemish Parliament, brought together in a plenary assembly, has to take a decision, such as the passing of a decree proposal or a bill, the Speaker asks the assembly to vote on it. If the majority of the members present (half plus one) votes for, the text in question is passed. If a majority votes against, it is rejected. Only in certain cases is an exceptional majority required such as two thirds of the votes cast.

The plenary assembly can vote on a submitted text in various ways. The simplest way is by sitting and standing up. In this case the Speaker first asks those 'for' to stand up, and then those 'against'. If the result is not immediately clear, then both groups are counted. This voting procedure is not permitted for all matters, however.

The most user-friendly method of voting is electronic polling. Each member has a panel on his desk with a green button for a 'yes' vote, a red for 'no' and a white for abstention. The members push the appropriate button at the Speaker's request. The 'yes' votes then light up in green on the voting board at the left front of the Domed Hall, the 'no' votes red and the abstentions white. In this way the public and the press can check which way the individual MPs vote. Secret voting is only used in very exceptional circumstances. In order to cast valid polls or secret votes there must be a quorum, which means at least half the MPs must be present. Abstentions count in the quorum, but not in the majority of votes.

VOOR	080		VOOR	075
ONTH.	015		ONTH.	015
TEGEN	027		TEGEN	026
TOT.	122		TOT.	116

NR. 02

BEGIN STEMMING
EINDE STEMMING

VERWERKT

The distribution of seats in the Flemish Parliament after
the first direct elections on 21st May 1995

CVP	37
VLD	27
SP	26
VB	17
VU	9
AGALEV	7
UF	1
	124

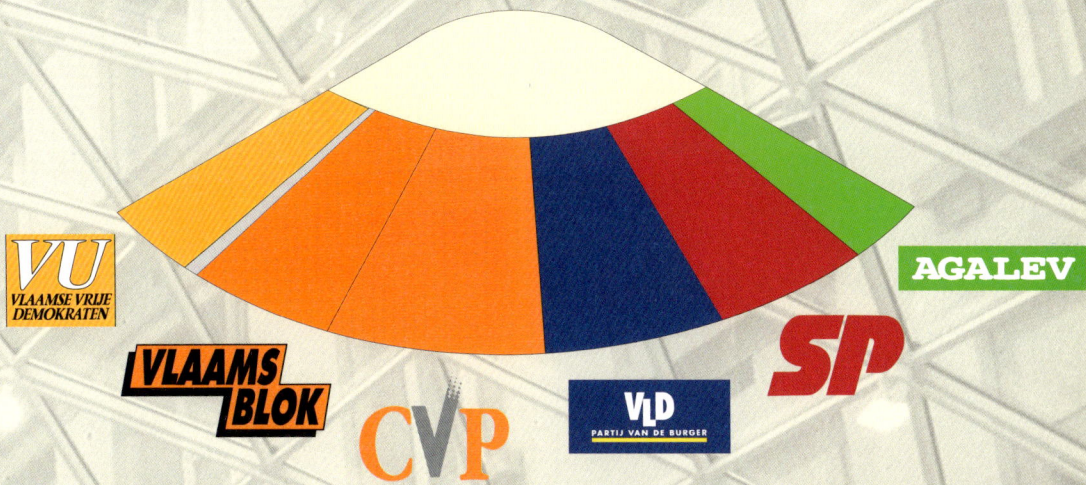

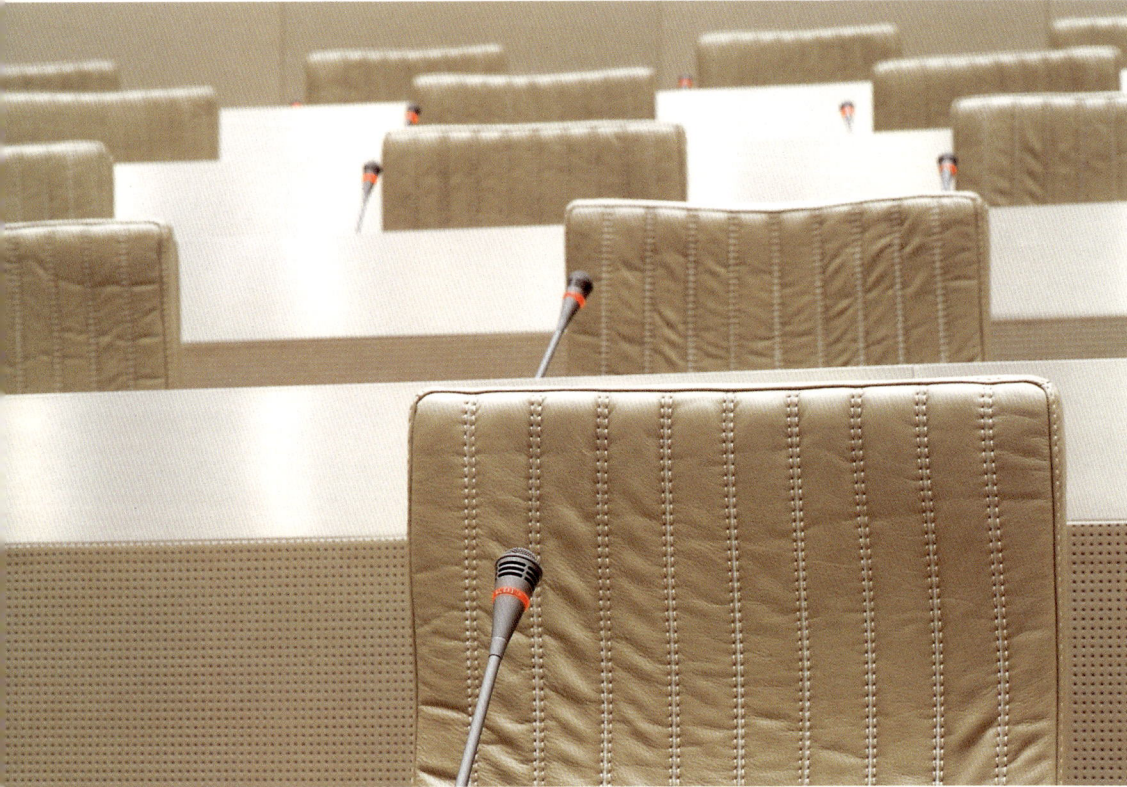

THE FLEMISH PARLIAMENT APPROVES DECREES

A Flemish policy with Flemish decrees

The Flemish people are possibly not always aware that the Flemish Parliament takes decisions regarding major aspects of the daily life. It determines to a great extent the society we shall be living in tomorrow. For instance, it determines how Flemish education is organized, how we will tackle pollution, how we are to take care of the growing number of pensioners and which direction we want to take in environmental planning, to give just a few examples. The Flemish Parliament occupies itself with those aspects of policy that concern the citizen most closely.

Flemish policy is shaped by the approval of *decrees*, which are Flemish laws applying to all Flemish people and which they must all observe. The Flemish Parliament can pass decrees in all the areas in which it has competence. The number of areas of competence was systematically increased by the state reforms of 1970, 1980, 1988 and 1993. The Flemish Parliament currently has competence in the areas of language use in Flanders and parts or all of the following sectors: culture, education, economy, employment and energy policy, environmental planning, housing and land use, environment and water policy, public works and transport and scientific policy. The Flemish Parliament can also use decrees to regulate so-called 'person-linked' affairs such as youth protection, family policy and child care, policy for the handicapped, equal opportunities policy and the integration of immigrants. It also has competence for the administrative supervision of the Flemish municipalities, provinces and inter-urban utility companies.

The initiative to issue a decree may come from either the Flemish Government or one of the members of the Flemish Parliament. In the first case it is called a *bill* and in the second a *decree proposal*. So we might say that the Flemish Parliament and Government prepare Flemish policies together.

In practice it is even the case that more bills are passed than proposals. This is because, among other things, the Flemish Government, in preparing bills, has administrative departments with more than 10,000 civil servants at its disposal, whereas Flemish MPs have to rely on themselves, the staff of the parliamentary parties and the limited staff of the Flemish Parliament.

The Flemish Parliament aims to be as closely involved with the preparation of bills as possible. This is why the minister-president of the Flemish Government presents an exhaustive policy document to the Flemish Parliament at the start of each new session. This policy document announces how policy will be pursued in the various areas of competence. And every year all the ministers write one or more policy letters in which they explain the policy for their own areas of competence in more detail. For example, the minister who has authority over education writes an Education Policy Letter, and so forth. These policy letters are discussed at length in the relevant committees of the Flemish Parliament.

How a decree comes into being

At the moment a bill or a decree proposal is submitted to the Flemish Parliament, the Speaker judges whether it is admissible. It must concern a matter for which the Flemish Parliament has competence, and must not be in conflict with the Belgian Constitution.

The Bureau then refers it to a *committee*. Parliamentary committees are the parliament's specialist working bodies.

They are what one might call 'mini-parliaments', each composed of fifteen permanent and fifteen acting members, composed in proportion to the strengths

Parliamentary committees

The Flemish Parliament currently has thirteen committees that meet regularly:

Committee for Internal Affairs, Urban Renewal and Housing
Committee for Foreign and European Affairs
Committee for Culture and Sport
Committee for Financial and Budgetary Matters
Committee for Environment and Nature Conservation Issues
Committee for Media Policy
Committee for Education, Training and Science and Research Policy
Committee for Procedures and Co-operation
Committee for Town and Country Planning, Public Works and Transport
Committee for State Reform and General Affairs
Committee for Legal Proceedings
Committee for Public Welfare, Health and Family Affairs
Committee for Employment and Economic Affairs

There is a separate committee called the Interparliamentary Committee for the Dutch Language Union. It consists of eleven members of the Flemish Parliament and eleven members of the States General, the Dutch Parliament. Flanders and the Netherlands cooperate in the Language Union, which was established in 1980, to develop and promote the Dutch language and literature. One of the topics discussed by this committee was the new spelling.

The Advisory and Consulting Committee for Brussels and Flemish Brabant deliberate on affairs specific to Brussels and Flemish Brabant.

The committee meetings have in principle been open to the public since the change in regulations made on 10th June 1966.

The Hans Memling Room

The Antoon Van Dyck Room, one of the largest committee rooms.

of the parliamentary parties. MPS who are not members of the committee can attend the discussions but do not have voting rights.

There are currently thirteen committees, each specialized in particular matters. So, for instance, a bill or decree proposal regarding education will be discussed in the Education, Training and Science and Research Committee.

The committees study the text of the bill or proposal together with the relevant minister. The text can still be changed – *amended* – during the com-

The James Ensor Room

mittee's discussions if a majority of the members agrees. A committee can also arrange *hearings* in order to find out more about the content of a bill or proposal. To close the discussions a vote is taken on the bill or proposal. When discussions start the committee appoints a reporter who, together with the committee's official secretary, writes a summarized report of the meetings.

The final vote on the bill or proposal is taken in the *plenary assembly*, the highest organ of the Flemish Parliament. The Brussels Flemings, who belong to the Flemish Community but not to the Flemish Region, do not take part in the vote on bills and proposals concerning regional affairs.

When a bill or proposal is passed by the plenary assembly, it still has to be ratified by the Flemish Government. The decree is then published, with a French translation, in the Belgian Law Gazette. As soon as a decree is published and becomes operative, all Flemish citizens are expected to be aware of and comply with it.

Narcisse Tordoir's 'Untitled' gives the Pieter Brueghel Room a very special atmosphere. The work consists of thirty-two strictly ordered small multicoloured panels, each with a different motif on a black and white background.

THE FLEMISH PARLIAMENT APPROVES THE BUDGET

One of the most important parliamentary prerogatives concerns the right to approve the budget. By this means the parliament makes the necessary financial resources available to the government to implement the proposed policy.

The Flemish Government needs a lot of financial resources to be able to implement a good Flemish policy. One only has to think of the financing of education, care for the handicapped and the building of cultural and sports centres. Every year the Flemish Parliament decides how much to make available to the Flemish Government, and in which sectors these resources are to be spent. To this end it passes two *budgetary decrees*: decrees containing all the revenues and expenditure for the coming calendar year. The passing of these decrees is preceded by extensive budget discussions in the Flemish Government and the various parliamentary committees.

Flanders is still to a great extent dependent for its income on the resources the federal state makes available. It has itself only limited powers of taxation. In this sense the reform of the Belgian state remains incomplete. In a fully federal state the member states are able to generate their own revenue much more than is currently possible in Belgium.

THE FLEMISH PARLIAMENT MONITORS THE FLEMISH GOVERNMENT

An important part of the day to day work of the Flemish MPs is to monitor the work of the Flemish Government. The Flemish Parliament keeps a constant eye on whether the government is not betraying the trust put in it. In order to do this it has several parliamentary means of control.

MPS can put a *spoken question* to a minister in both the plenary assembly and the committees. The question and its answer, intended to obtain information, must only take up a few minutes and must concern a topical problem.

MPS can also send ministers a *written question*, to which the minister must reply within twenty days. Both the question and the answer are published in the parliament's *Bulletin of Questions and Answers*. But if the minister allows this period to expire by more than ten days, the written question is, at the request of the MP who submitted it, transposed into a spoken question, which will immediately be put on the agenda.

This question system enables the practical applications of and the difficulties of interpreting decrees to be discussed with the relevant ministers.

Press rooms

The press has an important part to play in a modern democracy. This is why the press is sometimes also called the fourth estate. It is essential that the printed and audiovisual press have all the facilities they need in the Flemish Parliament building to keep the public informed of its day-to-day operations.

The Flemish Parliament currently has forty accredited journalists. This means they can use the press facilities in the Flemish Parliament at any time. There are special boxes and work rooms for the press in the Domed Hall. The journalists from both the printed press and the audiovisual media have every facility at their disposal there – even data communication lines – to send their reports and comments as quickly as possible. There are special boxes for the television cameras.

An MP who wishes to bring up a broader problem for discussion can make an *interpellation*. The interpellator can call upon the minister to justify himself in connection with actions he has performed or neglected to perform. An interpellation can be made in either the plenary assembly or a committee. It usually expands into a wider debate in which all MPs may participate. The right of interpellation gives the opposition the opportunity to put one or more ministers through the mill in public.

If the minister's answer does not satisfy the interpellator or another MP, he can propose a *motion of no-confidence*. Such a motion signifies a rejection of the policy of the minister or the government. If such a motion is passed by a majority of MPs, the minister will resign or the government fall. In this case they must be replaced by a new minister or a new government.

The interpellator or any other MP may also limit themselves to a recommendation. He may then propose a *substantiated motion*. If this type of motion is passed by a majority, it constitutes a significant political signal. The

The Frans Masereel Room, the room for press conferences, where no one will lose their direction...

government is expected to take account of the Flemish Parliament's recommendation.

In addition to this, the Flemish Parliament has the *right of enquiry*: it can set up a parliamentary committee of enquiry with judicial authority. In 1993, one such committee of enquiry investigated the spending of the government subsidies intended for the closing of the coal mines in the Kempen area.

The annual *budgetary discussions* are also a time of major political control. If a parliamentary group does not approve the budget, it is thereby also rejecting the policy pursued.

The leadership of the Flemish Parliament: Speaker, Bureau and Extended Bureau

The day-to-day administration of the Flemish Parliament – a large organization with a specific task: practising politics – is no sinecure. All the Flemish MPs, whether they belong to the majority or the opposition, must be able to play a part in the political forum. For this reason all the parliamentary parties are involved in the leadership of the Flemish Parliament.

At the start of every session, on the fourth Monday in September, the plenary assembly elects a *Speaker, four Deputy Speakers* and *three Secretaries*, who together form the executive committee or *Bureau*. These appointments are made in accordance with the rule of proportional representation, which means that in principle all the parliamentary parties are represented in the Bureau. But in practice the appointment of the Speaker of the Flemish Parliament is not a purely parliamentary matter: this appointment forms part of the political agreement reached by the majority parties when the Flemish Government is formed at the beginning of the session. This is a custom the opposition parties do not very much appreciate.

The Speaker assumes the most important political tasks of the Flemish Parliament. He chairs the full assembly meetings, assesses the admissibility of the items submitted, watches over the observance of the regulations, is responsible for the implementation of all decisions taken by the parliament, Bureau and Extended Bureau and represents the parliament in the outside world. The Speaker has the specific task of remaining strictly impartial. In terms of protocol, the Speaker of the Flemish Parliament is Flanders' first citizen.

The publications of the Flemish Parliament

Since 1971 the Flemish parliamentary assembly has published four major series of documents.

The Proceedings contain the full text of the speeches made in the plenary assembly. Since the Proceedings are only published after several weeks, a Summary Report is also published immediately after each plenary assembly. The bills and decree proposals, amendments and other printed parliamentary texts together form the so-called Articles. And finally there is the Bulletin of Questions and Answers, a collection of the written questions put by MPs to ministers, with the ministers' replies.

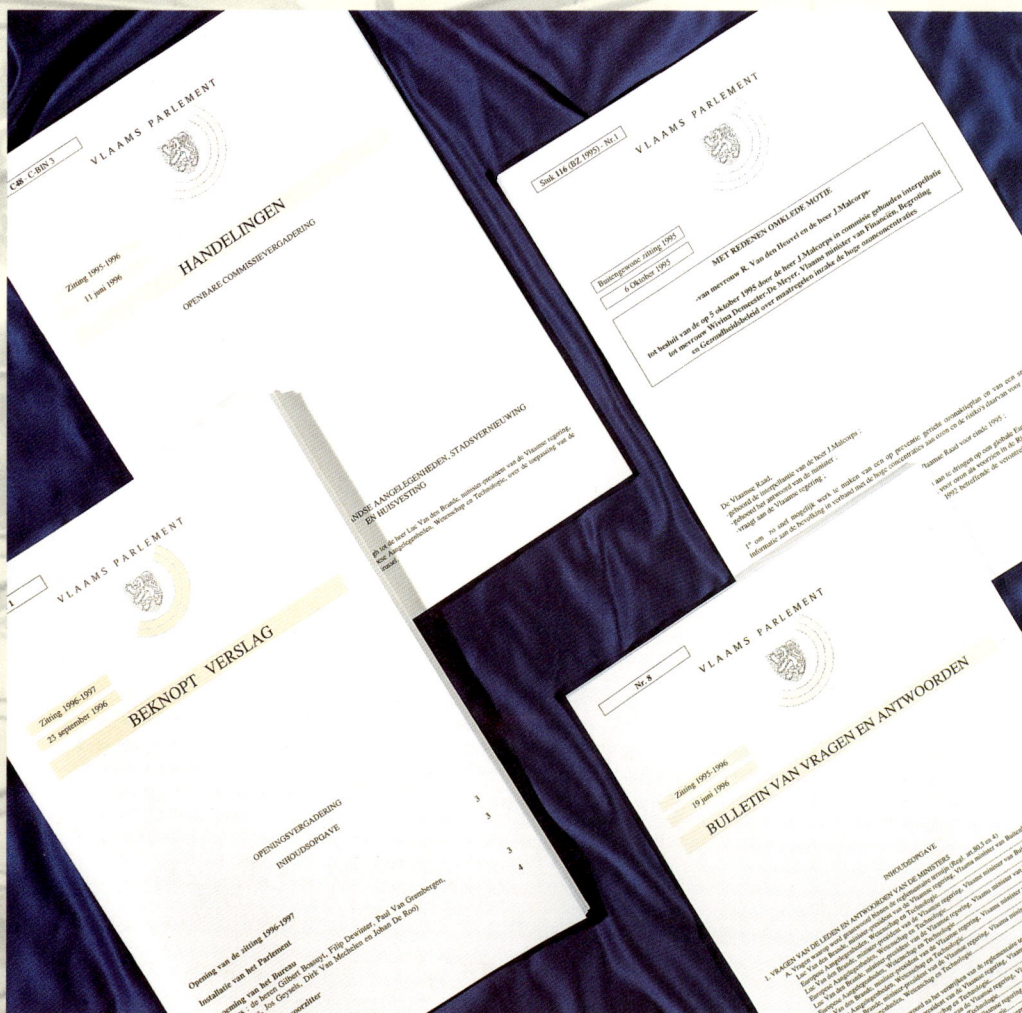

Details of the restored Speaker's office.

In the exercise of his duties the Speaker is assisted by the Bureau and if necessary the Extended Bureau, which he also chairs. The *Bureau* meets very often and takes important decisions of an administrative and organizational nature regarding staff matters, maintenance of the buildings and budgetary matters. The Bureau is expanded by the addition of the chairmen of the recognized parliamentary parties when it comes to the organization of purely political matters such as fixing the dates and the agenda of the plenary assembly meetings. This is then called the *Extended Bureau*.

The departments of the Flemish Parliament provide the political organization with administrative support and see to the implementation of decisions made by the Speaker, the Bureau and the Extended Bureau. The parliamentary departments are headed by a *Registrar* with the rank of secretary general, who is appointed from outside the parliament by the plenary assembly. The Flemish Parliament at present employs about 190 civil servants, divided between the Secretary General's office, the Director General's office, the Department of External Relations and the boards responsible for Legislation, Information, Studies and Advice, and Internal Administration and Logistics.

In addition to this, the Flemish MPs can also call on their personal staff and the staff of their parliamentary party.

The typical profile of the Flemish Parliament in a federal Belgium

As was shown in chapter 1, federal Belgium has five other parliaments apart from the Flemish Parliament. The federal parliament, comprising the Chamber of Flemish People's Representatives (MPs) and the Senate, passes laws that apply to all Belgians, such as those regarding defence and justice. The parliaments of the French Community, the German-speaking Community and the Walloon Region pass decrees for the members of the French Community (including the French-speaking institutions in Brussels), the German-speaking Community and Wallony respectively. And finally, the Brussels parliament, officially called the Brussels Capital Council, issues orders for the Brussels Region.

The recent past has demonstrated that the regional parliaments do not necessarily pursue similar policies. It is clear, for example, that in terms of education, the parliament of the French Community takes political options different to those of the Flemish Parliament, which immediately explains why the Flemish and French-speaking educational systems are growing further and further apart. This development is part and parcel of the logic of the federal model.

It is clear that in the future the regional parliaments will increasingly choose their own political direction, so that paths followed by the various communities and regions will differ much more than is the case today. In this respect the Flemish Parliament has already proven its individuality: between 1971 and 1996 Flanders slowly but surely acquired a social identity of its own in the framework of the Belgian state.

However, the Flemish Parliament does not want to present itself as a characteristically Flemish parliament only in terms of policy. The way it organizes its work has already shown that when it comes to its operation it also wishes to assume its own characteristically Flemish face. It is distancing itself from old and often less fortunate customs that had evolved in the unitary parliament, and it intends to promote a new political culture in Flanders: open and transparent politics, rising above the sterile political game of majority versus opposition, and which should make the Flemish Parliament a model of a modern and efficiently working parliament. Measures taken recently such as public access to committee meetings, working visits in the field and closer involvement of the Flemish Parliament in the work of policy preparation are just a few examples of the efforts made to give concrete form to this new political culture.

A logical consequence of the process of federalization that started in 1970 is that the areas of competence of the member states will continue to increase in the future. The political parties on the two sides of the language border are growing apart, and the direct election of the regional parliaments is setting a new community dynamism in motion. The most recent examples of this are the debate on the regionalization of social security and the fiscal autonomy of the member states.

The Flemish Parliament will in the future undoubtedly play an even more important part than is the case today. Considering the fresh and rejuvenating wind currently whistling through the Flemish Parliament building, and remembering the many difficulties the Flemish parliamentary assembly has successfully overcome in the recent past, Flanders may look forward to the future with some confidence. New and as yet unknown challenges will never be too great.

The Flemish Parliament visitors entrance on the Leuvenseweg.

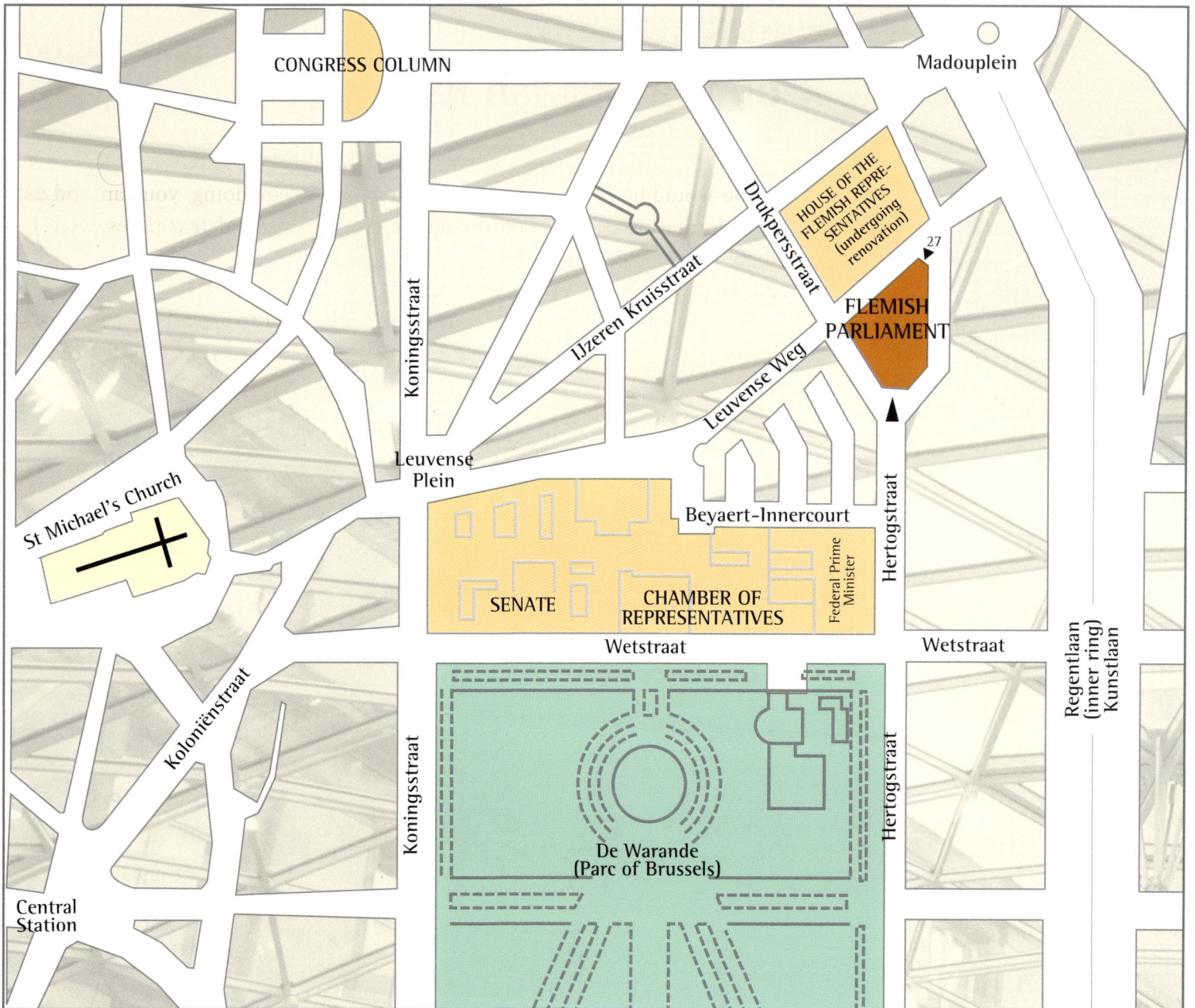

CONGRESS COLUMN

Madouplein

HOUSE OF THE FLEMISH REPRE-SENTATIVES (undergoing renovation)

27

FLEMISH PARLIAMENT

Koningsstraat

IJzeren Kruisstraat

Drukpersstraat

Leuvense Weg

Leuvense Plein

St Michael's Church

Beyaert-Innercourt

Hertogstraat

SENATE

CHAMBER OF REPRESENTATIVES

Federal Prime Minister

Wetstraat

Wetstraat

Regentlaan (inner ring) Kunstlaan

Koloniënstraat

Koningsstraat

Hertogstraat

De Warande (Parc of Brussels)

Central Station

Practical information on the Flemish Parliament

If you would like to know what the Flemish MPs are doing, you can find useful information everyday on the public broadcaster's *Teletext* pages. Page 775 shows the agenda of the plenary meeting of the Flemish Parliament. Page 776 shows the agenda of the committees.

If you wish to see your Flemish MP at work, you can attend a *plenary meeting* or *committee meeting*. The Flemish Parliament is an open house. If there is a meeting taking place, all you have to do is apply at the reception desk at the visitors' entrance, Leuvenseweg 27 in Brussels. There is no need to book.

If you want to know what views your MP is expressing in the Flemish Parliament, you can read the *publications of the Flemish Parliament*. You can take out an *annual subscription* to them. The Summary Report costs 500 BEF a year. The Proceedings cost 1000 BEF a year. The Bulletin of Questions and Answers costs 1000 BEF per year. Simply transfer the correct amount to the Flemish Parliament, Abonnementenbeheer (Subscription Administration), 1011 Brussels, account number 000-0724244-42. Write clearly which publications you wish to receive.

If you would like a *guided tour* of the Flemish Parliament building, you can apply for a *group visit*. A guided tour offers you a detailed explanation of the way the Flemish Parliament works and the structure of our democracy. You can get an application form for a group visit from the Flemish Parliament's External Relations Department (tel: (02)552 11 11, fax: (02)513 74 80). Please remember that a guided tour must be applied for two months in advance. Call beforehand to make sure the date you have in mind is still available.

Technical specifications of the Flemish Parliament building

CONTRACTOR: FLEMISH PARLIAMENT & BUILDING DIRECTORATE
WORKING PARTY FOR THE HOUSING OF THE FLEMISH PARLIAMENT

Chairmen

Frans Grootjans, Jean Pede, Louis Vanvelthoven, Eddy Baldewijns,
Norbert De Batselier

Members

Ward Beysen, André De Beul, Alfons Laridon, Marc Olivier, Eric Pinoie,
Luc Van Nieuwenhuysen

Coordination and Technical Inspection	Building Directorate
Architecture and Interior Design	Jozef Fuyen,
	Fuyen Architects/Antwerp
	Willy Verstraete,
	Arrow Engineers/Ghent
Stability study	Peeters Engineers/Hasselt
Electricity study	Ingenium NV/Bruges
Heating, Ventilation and Cooling study	Talboom Engineers/Puurs
Lift study	Varendonck Group/Ghent
Acoustic study	Prof. G. Vermeir/KUL
	Cauberg and Verbeemen/Hasselt
	Johan Delaere/Antwerp
Structural work, windows,	
* dome for assembly hall*	NV Cordeel/Temse
Finishing and sanitary facilities	NV Van Laere/Burcht
Restoration	Vandekerckhove NV/Ingelmunster
Fixed and movable furnishings	Potteau Labo/Kortrijk-Heule
Control system	Landis & Gyr NV/Brussels
Power supply	ENI NV/Aartselaar
Telephone installations	Philips Professional Systems NV/Brussels
Sound & Voting installation	CEI Electrotec NV/Zaventem
Security installation	Ditech bvba/Aalst
Video system	Philips Professional Systems NV/Brussels
HVAC installation	Daeninck & Deweerdt bvba/Bruges
Lifts	Schindler NV/Brussels
Communications	Alcatel BBS & ICN/Zaventem
Curtains	Servio NV/Roeselaere

Bibliography

CHAPTER 1

Main works

GOOSSENS, M., *Ontstaan en groei van het Vlaams Parlement, 1970-1995.*
Brussels/Kapellen, 1995.

Other works

DEDEURWAERDER, J., 'De kulturele autonomie: een ontgoochelend experiment'. In: *Vlaanderen Morgen,* 1980, pp. 21-29.

PEDE, J., 'De Vlaamse Raad: terugblik en bezinning'. In: *De Vlaamse Gids,* 1983, pp. 69-75.

RIMANQUE, K., 'Wordt de twintigjarige Vlaamse Raad meerderjarig ?'
In: *Ons Erfdeel,* vol.34, 1991, pp. 681-690.

VANDEKERCKHOVE, R., 'De groei van de cultuurautonomie in België: van idee tot instelling'. In: *Tijdschrift voor Bestuurswetenschappen en Publiekrecht,* vol. 27, 1972, pp. 235-242.

VAN IMPE, H., *De Cultuurraad voor de Nederlandse cultuurgemeenschap.*
Brussels, 1973.

VAN IMPE, H. & BAETEMAN, M., *De Vlaamse Raad. Het ontstaan, de groei en de betekenis van het Vlaamse parlement.* Antwerp, 1985.

CHAPTERS 2 & 3

Main works

BRAEKEN, J., 'Het Vlaams Parlement'. In: *Monumenten en Landschappen,* vol. 15, no. 2, 1996, pp. 21-44.

BRAL, G.J., *Concert Noble.* Brussels, 1990.

Other works

BRAL, G.J., 'De Waux-Hall in Brussel'. In: *Monumenten en Landschappen,* vol. 5, no. 3, 1986, pp. 35-53.

CELIS, M.M., De egyptiserende maçonnieke tempels van de Brusselse loges 'Les Amis Philanthropes' en 'Les Vrais Amis de l'Union et de Progrès Réunis'. In: *Monumenten en Landschappen,* vol. 3, no. 3, 1984, pp. 25-41.

VAN DE STEENE, W., *Het Paleis der Natie.* Brussels, 1981.

VICTOIR, J. & VANDERPERREN, J., *Hendrik Beyaert. Van classicisme tot Art Nouveau.* St Martens Latem, 1992.

WAUTERS, A. & HENNE, A., *Histoire de la Ville de Bruxelles (nouvelle édition du texte original de 1845, augmentée de nombreuses reproductions de documents choisis par M. Martens, archiviste de la ville).* Brussels, 1975, 4 vols.

CHAPTER 4

Vlaams Parlement. Brussels, Vlaams Parlement, s.d. (booklet).

Sources of illustrations and photographs

Illustrations

p. 32   Arrow Engineers, Ghent.

pp. 48-49   Print by Lucas Vorstermans Jr., 1659 (Österreichische Nationalbibliothek, Vienna, Blaeau-Van der Hem Atlas).

pp. 50-51   Plan drawn up by Joachim Zinner, dated to 1779. (State Archives, Brussels, maps and plans in manuscript 41).

pp. 52-53   State Archives, Brussels, maps and plans in manuscript 520.

pp. 59   Académie Royale de Bruxelles, Brussels Art Library, Beyaert Trust, plan 46.

p. 61   Travaux d'architecture exécutés en Belgique par Henri Beyaert, 11, Ministère des Chemins de fer, plan 1.

p. 62   Académie Royale de Bruxelles, Brussels Art Library, Beyaert Trust, plan 13.

p. 63   Académie Royale de Bruxelles, Brussels Art Library, Beyaert Trust, plan 35.

p. 64   Académie Royale de Bruxelles, Brussels Art Library, Beyaert Trust, plan 8.

p. 65   Brussels Municipal Archives, Public Works, dossier 10.331.

pp. 74-76   Arrow Engineers, Ghent.

Photographs

Marnix Van Esbroeck, *except the following:*

pp. 29, 34-35   Joris Luyten.

pp. 56-57, 60   Oswald Pauwels.

pp. 68, 69   Museum of Post and Telecommunications, Brussels.

Imprint

Photography

MARNIX VAN ESBROECK

Editor

MARTINE GOOSSENS

Coordination

KRIS VAN ESBROECK

Design

STUDIO LANNOO

Research

MARTINE GOOSSENS (chapter 1)

JO BRAEKEN (chapter 2)

JO LEFEBURE (chapter 3)

Language advice

JORIS DEDEURWAERDER

Translator

GREGORY BALL

© Uitgeverij Lannoo, Tielt

D/1997/45/244 - ISBN 90 209 3281 0

Printed and bound by

Drukkerij Lannoo, Tielt - 1997

Printed in Belgium